JOCELYN DETTLOFF

IT RAINED
IN THE DESERT

one woman's story
of spirit and resilience

It Rained in the Desert: One Woman's Story of Spirit and Resilience
Copyright © 2013 Jocelyn Dettloff
in association with faithAlivebooks

Some names have been changed to protect identities.
The cover photo was taken April 13, 1997, the morning of the
accident in Soussesvlei, Namibia.

Interior Design by Kate Budzynski
Cover Design by Christa Blackman

ISBN 978-0-9764221-6-7

faithAlivebooks.com
spiritual and religious books

Grand Rapids, Michigan
pierson.dj@gmail.com

For my Mother,
Thank you for everything.

IT RAINED
IN THE DESERT

"I wish the ring had never come to me. I wish none of this had happened."

"So do all who live to see such times. But that is not for them to decide. All we have to decide is what to do with the time that is given to us. There are other forces at work in this world…"

—Frodo Baggins and Gandalf the Grey
from the movie *Lord of the Rings, Fellowship of the Ring*.

CHAPTER ONE
IT RAINED IN THE DESERT

"Your daughter has been in an accident," began the telephone call to my mother in Kalamazoo, Michigan on Sunday, April 13, 1997 at about 9:30 PM. Shocking, heart-stopping words every parent dreads. "She's alive, but..." The insurance representative began giving my mother some details, but abruptly put her on hold to make sure he conveyed the correct facts. He had information on two American women injured in separate accidents, but in close proximity. One sustained more severe injuries than the other. Without knowing the full extent of my injuries or what precisely happened, Mom felt a miniscule sense of relief knowing I was still alive.

Prior to the phone call, Mom had gone about her nightly rituals on an ordinary Sunday evening. The insurance company had tried calling numerous times that day, but left no messages on the answering machine. Mom had gone shopping, nearly all day, with my sister, Gretchen. Mom then busied herself with getting ready for bed and organizing things for work the next day. Hearing the phone ring, she had casually answered it, thinking it was my sister. Instead it was the phone call that brought life to a screeching halt. She heard the crushing news and sank into the desk chair by the phone.

While she waited during the long silence, my mother

started praying that I was not the one with more extensive injuries. At last the insurance representative returned to the line, "Yes, I do have the details correct. It is Jocelyn with more severe injuries. She is paralyzed and cannot walk…" And he went on to report all the information available at the time.

Unfortunately, my mother could not dash down to the hospital to see me or speak to me immediately on the phone. I was thousands of miles away on the other side of the world in Namibia, Africa. My accident had occurred thirteen hours earlier at 12:00 noon Greenwich Mean Time.

** ** ** ** ** **

My journey began with a rustic overland camping trip starting in Nairobi, Kenya in February 1997. I had travelled there from Kalamazoo by myself to meet the other people from different parts of the world who had signed up to experience the same adventure. The trip was to take us through Kenya, Tanzania, Malawi, Zambia, Zimbabwe, Botswana, Namibia, and finally to Cape Town, South Africa to conclude the journey in May. This would not be a mission or service-related trip. Instead it would be purely a holiday to hang out, have fun, see the countries and their animals in the wild, and revel in cultures completely different than our own. I was the only American in our group of 20. Others came from England, Australia, Norway and Canada, to name but a few.

We brought along a sleeping bag, clothes and a roll mat;

expedition furnished all our other supplies. Our truck was unlike anything I had ever seen before. The best way to describe it would be as a big dump truck with enough seating for 22 people, similar to a commercial coach, but not quite as luxurious. It stored the cooking and camping equipment, a water tank with purified drinking water, a small refrigerator (for the beer, of course) and had room enough for rucksacks and luggage. This rustic, roughing it sort of trip did not cater to those who liked more creature comforts. We spent

Dragoman Overland Trucks, courtesy of Dragoman

some long days riding around on the truck. We also went on game drives in the national parks and observed wildlife in its natural habitat. What an extraordinary gift to observe elephants and giraffes in the rough.

On April 12 we arrived at our campground in Sessriem, Namibia. Namibia is a long country just above South Africa beside the Atlantic Ocean on the west coast. A stunning, vast, primarily desert country, Namibia holds some of the oldest and largest sand dunes in the world. The country measures about the size of Texas and Louisiana, with a population of about two million people. It also contains the Etosha national park, the third largest in Africa.

Once off the truck and after a visit to the toilet blocks, we did our usual tasks of unloading the rucksacks, pitching our tents and that evening's cook team staring to prepare dinner. Without the modern day electronic devices to consume

Pitching my tent at Sessriem

our attention, after dinner people often gathered around the campfire. Feeling a bit tired and not very social, I sat in the tent writing in my journal. Sometimes I felt very social and other times craved a bit of quiet time. I went to bed on the early side because the next morning we were headed to Sossusvlei, a place with some of the largest sand dunes in the world. Had I known what the next day had in store for me, I would have joined my fellow travelers around the campfire to have a beer, laugh with my fellow travelers and feel the heat of the fire on my shins.

The next day, Sunday, April 13 started early so we could arrive at the dunes before sunrise and watch the sun come up over them. It was still pitch dark when we awoke. Sleepily I walked to the toilet block. When coming back to the truck, the most extraordinary scene lay before me. In the distance behind the truck, heat lightning periodically illuminated the sky with huge, zigzag bolts. Someone stood on top of the truck and this small person on the truck contrasted greatly with the vast sky and huge bolts of lightning. I stopped to absorb this awesome sight and was filled with respect for its powerful beauty. It remains etched in my memory. A real Kodak moment, but I did not happen to bring a camera with me to the toilet.

The morning air was cool. Despite being in the desert region of Namibia, the nights could get cool. Not cold enough for long pants and sweatshirts but pushing the comfort zone of shorts and a T-shirt. When we arrived at Sossusvlei it was cloudy, a bit chilly and windy. Disappointment hung in the air since the whole point of getting up in the pre-dawn hours was to see the sun peek over the dunes. However, as the sun began to rise, the clouds started breaking apart. Although we did not have a chance to see all the colors change as the sunlight hit the dunes and sand from different angles (as I had imagined they would), the sight still possessed breathtaking beauty.

With the sun up, we had a few free hours to wander in the dunes before heading back to the campground. Paula, Margaret, Matt and I took off to explore. All three were from England. Matt was in his late 20's and one of the drivers for the trip. A Kiefer Sutherland/Kurt Cobain look-alike who worked in the central London finance sector, he got laid off (made redundant as the Brits say) when the economy started a downturn in the 90's. Paula, who would be turning 30 on the trip, signed up for the same three-month segment as I. We became tent mates for the trip and good friends. Paula also worked in London for a finance broker and had wanted to take an adventurous holiday. Margaret was in her 40's and of Caribbean descent. While happily married, her husband remained in England and she took on the full 9-month overland challenge by herself. She had boarded the truck in England, journeyed down through Europe, down the Ivory Coast and would conclude her expedition in Cape Town. Her husband flew down to see her at various times during her trip. I admired her for being so independent.

The Namib Desert had seen an unusual amount of rain that year. As a result desert flowers and greenery grew in abundance. The dry parched ground had soaked in all the water, leaving it quite muddy until the sun came out and dried it up. Vast areas looked like the base of a parched mud puddle, carrying on and on into the distance. We walked, skipped and jumped on the dried cracked ground. Stepping on larger pieces generated this thud/breaking sound causing a vibrating sensation to travel through my legs and body as the pieces broke apart under my weight. Stepping on the smaller pieces was like walking on egg shells and had much more crackle than the big ones. The impulse to move from piece to piece stomping around is the same as the urge to pop, jump on and twist bubble wrap—to hear the sound and feel the POP!

Paula and I

Part of the group trudged far into the park to see some of the largest sand dunes in the world—as tall as 300 meters (900 feet). It was over a mile's walk through loose sand to get there. The four of us couldn't be bothered, especially with so many other dunes so near. So we passed the time charging up and down the mammoth dunes in closer proximity. Frozen in my memory are the perfect peaks at the top of the dune where both sides meet. A perfect squaring as both sides came together. We came and messed it all up. However, when left alone, it re-formed back to that perfect angle. This experience truly illustrated how the human imprint can ruin nature completely, but when left to itself, nature will achieve perfection.

After playing, jumping and filling our shoes (not to mention just about everywhere else on our bodies) with sand, the four of us meandered back to the truck to wait for the others to return. By this time, the sun was out in full force and starting to heat up the day. You know you are in Africa when you have to put on sunscreen at 8:00 AM to avoid getting burned.

As we waited, a tour bus pulled in and 60- and 70-year-old tourists lumbered down the steps with cameras hanging round their necks, wearing high white socks and hats. It was then that I had an epiphany, my own little "A-ha!" moment. I realized how lucky I was to be doing this trip in my youth. My friends back home envied me because of my freedom and all the places I traveled. I pitied all the Americans who would wait until their "golden years" and retirement to see such sites. These older people would not be running up and down the dunes and feeling the sand cascade away beneath their feet like us as we charged down the dunes. So thrilling, so invigorating. They only saw the dunes, but we experienced them. I expect many aspects of their trip, in comparison to mine, were like that—passive viewing vs. diving in with gusto. The I-saw-the-movie experience rather than the-sucking-marrow-out-of-life experience.

By now, most people in the group had returned and everyone grabbed a seat on the truck and we headed back to the campground. Along the way, we stopped at a dune to go sledding. In Namibia, they called it sand boarding. This was before the introduction of the stand-up device similar to a snowboard for snow hills. The drivers, Meg and Matt, had chosen the dune. Meg, the lead driver for the trip, was a blonde, long-haired, spunky, cute Australian woman. Always chipper, chatty and very organized. A good contrast to Matt who was much more quiet and subdued.

The drivers for these overland trips are well trained, especially those who work for Dragoman, the company I chose. They go to Drago headquarters in Suffolk, England for thorough, comprehensive training. Each truck carries manuals and the drivers rely on the notes, stories and recommendations of other drivers. Never having been to this part of Namibia, Meg and Matt selected the dune based on what other Drago drivers had to say. It was called, quite simply, Dune 45 because it was 45 kilometers from the entrance of the park. The other drivers had prompted Meg and Matt to hang onto the sand boards we had used just a few days earlier in a town called Swakopmund.

Before arriving at Sessriem/Sossusvlei we had stayed a few days in Swakopmund which is surrounded by sand dunes. A local company took people sand boarding (sledding) and four-wheeling on the dunes. It sounded adventurous and fun, so at least half of us on the truck signed up to revel on the dunes of Swakopmund. Most in our group opted only for sand boarding. Matt, Paula and I comprised part of the five or so that opted to do both. The sand boards were made from the brown peg board material (minus the holes) hanging in garages and workshops around the world. It was cut into sheets about four feet long and two feet wide. The smooth side rested on the sand while the person lay on the rough side. To make it extra slick, we greased up the smooth side with furniture polish before setting it on the sand. The boards get so scratched up in one day that at the end of each day, the company chucks the boards. Knowing we would be in Sossusvlei in a few days (an excellent place for more sand boarding), Meg asked the Swakopmund folks if we could take some of the scratched up boards with us to use in Sossusvlei. They allowed us to take them since the boards were to be tossed anyway. We took about 10 and the sweethearts even threw in a tub of furniture polish.

We arrived at Dune 45. The dunes in this area stood

Dune 45, courtesy of Dragoman

more individually and spread out rather than connected in a long row. The 160 meter (480 foot) dune dwarfed our truck parked next to it. The day blossomed, becoming very sunny and very windy. Not everyone wanted to go sledding. The ones who did, including me, grabbed a board, polished it up and started up the dune. It was tough going trudging up the dune. As I soon discovered, there was no easy way to carry the board up a dune, especially in the wind. It was too wide to carry under my arm like a surf board and too awkward to carry lengthwise in front or to the side (as if carrying a piece of poster board) because the wind would catch it and knock me over. Carrying it flat on my head turned out to be the most comfortable way, although tiring because it meant walking up hill (sand no less) with my arms above my head. Try it some time. It reminded me of sledding as a kid—all bundled up, head tilted back so I could see between the slit from the bottom of my hat and the top of my scarf covering my face and trudging up the hill I just sailed down anxious to go down again. A heck of a lot of work, but the payoff rush was worth it.

When we reached the top whoever led chose the best spot to start sledding. None of us, not even the person leading, had ever been down this dune. From where I stood, the spot looked good to me—steep and long. Matt headed down first. When going down on your stomach, you curl the front end of the board up so it does not get bogged down in the sand. Then you use your feet as a rudder to steer and dig your toes into the sand to slow yourself down. I watched Matt descend. Instead of some good sturdy shoes or boots (I wore hiking boots), he wore flimsy flip flops. As he neared the bottom he rolled/fell off his board and never made it all the way to the bottom. At that time I did not know he did it intentionally.

Two or three more guys went before me, but I paid no attention to how they finished. Being the thrill seeker, I stepped up as the first girl to go down and focused on my task at hand. I flung myself onto the board, curled up the front, pushed off, went about five feet and stopped. My board flooded with sand. Hell-bent on getting down the dune, I did not see the people at the bottom, frantically waving their arms, warning the rest of us to not come down. Oblivious to the signals, I picked up my board, walked back to the top of the dune, shook the sand off the board, brushed myself off, tossed my board down again, climbed on, curled up the front end even more this time and pushed off with some extra umph. I was away!!

I was engulfed in my element; flying down the dune, the wind whipping in my hair, feeling the adrenaline rush I know and love so well. As I picked up speed, I tried digging my toes in the sand to slow down, but the dune was pretty hard packed. When having difficulty slowing myself down, it dawned on me that perhaps I was going too fast. I knew I was going fast, maybe even as fast as I had on the biggest dune we descended in Swakopmund.

When sand boarding in Swakopmund, the company took people on the same dunes everyday. One staff person remained up top and one person manned the bottom with both yelling and coaching how to steer. They knew the nature and intricacies of the dunes and knew what to tell people. When we plunged down the biggest dune of the day, they said that people could top out at 70 or 80 kilometers per hour (which translates into 35 to 45 mph). On that large dune, sand boarders went down one dune and started to go up the side of another, so gravity naturally slowed them down, plus the entire ride was a smooth, sandy surface.

Being from Michigan and sledding down snow hills all my life, I thought sand would be no different. After all, I was the kid who, at five years old, experienced quite a sledding adventure. My friend and I, I in front, she in back, were seated on a sled with runners on the bottom that could be steered with one's feet—however I did not know the sled could be steered. Dad gave us a big push to get going. Somewhere near the top, my friend fell off, leaving me flying down the hill. Careening toward the bottom, my sled headed right for a group of people with two or three toboggans perpendicular to the hill (and to me). Without knowing how to steer, I sailed right over those toboggans, through the group of people and eventually slowed down—unharmed, unafraid, a bit surprised and ready to go again!

But Dune 45 differed immensely from any snow hill or dune in Swakopmund. No one in our group had been on this dune before. No one knew the sand's texture or how people would finish at the bottom. This dune simply flattened out and changed into a rock and gravel surface, so our sleds moved from smooth sand to rocks and dirt. Like skating on ice then hitting sandpaper. Matt saw this early on and that is why he rolled himself off the board as he approached the bottom.

I did not. As I flew down the dune, only too late did I notice Meg and the others frantically waving their arms signaling me (and others) to slow down or not come down at all. I could not hear them yelling. I only heard wind rustling around me. But even though I tried, I could not slow down. Or maybe I was not digging in hard enough. From having descended the big dunes in Swakopmund, I knew I was reaching top speeds close to the 35 to 40 mph. As I approached the bottom I first thought my board would just stop on its own as the dune flattened out. Then I noticed I was heading for this mound of dirt and thought *this mound of dirt will stop me.* I hit it full on. My board stopped. I did not.

Upon impact, I flew off, somersaulted once or twice and sailed between 50 to 100 meters (150 to 300 feet) in the air. I vividly remember everything as I sped toward the mound of dirt. When I hit the mound, I knocked myself out and do not remember flying through the air. After hitting the mound, the next thing I remember is people calling my name and Keith holding my hand. Keith, from England, had joined our segment of the trip in Harare, Zimbabwe to meet up with his friend who boarded the truck in London for the nine-month African journey.

I was out cold for a few minutes, maybe even less than a minute. Groggily coming to, I first heard Keith's voice calling my name and felt him holding my hand. As I grew more alert, I noticed the numbness throughout the majority of my body—instant paralysis. After the millisecond it took for that information to register, I regained full consciousness. I felt absolutely nothing below my chest. Did I know right then and there I had broken my back and injured my spinal cord? No. Whatever had happened I just knew paralysis did not indicate anything good. Luckily, I was lucid and speaking. Meg and others discussed putting me back on the truck and taking me to the campground. I possessed the presence of mind to say, "No WAY!" While I did not know my exact injuries, I knew no one should be moving me.

Someone had to go for help. This situation was beyond the expertise of anyone present. No manual or book of notes on the truck could have prepared any driver for this scene. Matt climbed on the truck to go back to the campground. This was Africa...remote...vast...desert...Africa. No one knew how long it would take for help to come or exactly what kind of help would come. Thirty miles away down a dusty dirt road stood the campground. Waiting was the only thing to do.

Matt and an Australian guy took the truck while the others stayed with me. Before the truck left, Meg and a few others unloaded the cook tent from the truck to put something up around me for a bit of shelter. It was pretty windy at the bottom of the dune. Those sitting around me took turns holding my hand—Tierry from Switzerland, Kathy from Australia, Paula, my friend and tent mate, and Keith. He took the photograph on the cover of the book. He had captured a candid moment as I gazed across the dunes watching the sun rise the morning of my accident. Before Matt left, I remember him standing over me and my joking about us being two peas in a pod. A few days before in Swakopmund he had fallen, face first into the sidewalk and scraped up his nose quite badly.

People often ask me, "What was going through your mind? How did you react?" I experienced no panic, worry or fear. I felt very calm and tried to lie very still. I remained awake and lucid the entire time. I did not pass in and out of consciousness. No "what ifs" sailed through my mind. What was the point? I did not know precisely what happened. I focused my thoughts on the future, primarily for help to arrive and what the doctor would say.

Another popular question people ask is, "Were you in pain?" Surprisingly, no. One might expect excruciating pain with a broken back, or any type of broken bone. Not in this case, although I do think feeling "no pain" was more mind over matter. Of all things, remaining immobilized irritated me. However, my breathing became increasingly difficult. The paralysis started at my bra line and it felt like someone kept twisting a rubber band tighter and tighter around my chest at that line. Ever put a rubber band around your wrist or finger? At first it easily twists around, but eventually it gets harder to twist and all the added pressure with even one half twist can hurt. Since I wore a sports bra, we figured that cutting the band at the bottom a bit would relieve some of the pressure. Paula cut into the band, but the relief was minimal. I really concentrated on breathing in....and.... out....in....and......out. At this point no one, not even me, knew if I sustained any internal injuries. Did I puncture a lung or something else? My common sense and logic told me, *most likely, not. If you had, your breathing would have been difficult immediately.*

The minutes passed into hours. Early on, to pass the time people talked to me and kept asking me questions. Not knowing the extent of my injuries, they were most likely just trying to keep me awake. If I were to have a concussion, passing out or falling asleep would have been a bad sign. Time wore on and the conversation waned. What more could people say or ask, really? In such a precarious, potentially life-threatening situation people often start praying, even begging, "Please God, please don't let this be permanent. Please let help get here quickly. Please bring feeling back to my legs." But I did not. It is not because I did not believe in God—quite the opposite. I simply did not feel any panic or desperation that would warrant such pleas.

With the sun and the wind, I began to feel a bit parched and asked for my water bottle which, unfortunately, left with the truck. I always drank a ton of water. Paula and Matt always made fun of me because I would never be without my water bottle. I had a nifty little carrier to sling it across my shoulder and carry it with me like a bag. In Africa, you just never know when you are going to want a swig of water. And I like to be prepared. That bottle went just about everywhere with me. However, in this case, I did not think I would need it sledding down the dune. It figures, the one time I *really* wanted water and my bottle was nowhere in sight. Matt did leave a large container of water, but there was no easy way to get the water from the container to my lips.

The afternoon wore on. It had been bright and sunny when the accident happened, but now it started clouding up. Even with the cook tent semi-pitched around me, as the wind picked up, I had to keep my eyes closed because sand blew all over me. Paula leaned over me to shield my face with her long, brown, curly hair. When that grew tiresome, she put a shirt over my face to keep the sand away. At this point, my eyes were so encrusted with sand that I could not open them. Trying to brush away the sand and open my eyes would have been futile. You know how it is to get even one grain of sand in your eye. Even with the shirt over my face, blowing sand would have re-crusted my eyes anyway.

By now people grew quiet. What do you talk about when helplessly waiting in the middle of the desert to be rescued? I have no idea how much time passed. Drawn over by the group of people at the bottom of the dune, some tourists with their own cars stopped to investigate. One tourist was a doctor from Germany. He asked Meg a few questions. I do not remember hearing them speak or any part of their conversation. No one ever said, "You're paralyzed." People probably guessed what had happened, but no one dared state the obvious and discuss it. If no one said it aloud, then it would not be true, as though speaking would make it a reality, although I was lying right there in front of them unable to move.

The tourists headed back to our campground and offered to give others from the truck a lift back. People could wait with me and do nothing or go back to the campground and at least try to pass the time with a book, some writing or conversation. While the middle of nowhere with me meant no food or water, the campground at least had a little shop. Meg, Jean-Marie (from France), Tierry, Paula, Keith and Sal (from Australia, Oz for short) stayed. Sal's husband, Ross, had gone with Matt back to the campground for help.

With only a few of us left, the wind started picking up. The day once sunny and hot quickly turned gray and windy. Sand whipped through the air. The wind blew with enough force that everyone holding on had to bear down hard to support the protection around me. As the wind blew, rain started falling. The raindrops pelted my face and ceased just as quickly as they started. While the tent provided protection around my sides, it did not canopy over me for complete coverage. The shower was so brief, no one got drenched. Even though the desert received a lot of rain that year, I never would have thought, trudging up the sand dune, only a few hours earlier in the hot sun, that raindrops would later torpedo me while lying at the bottom of the dune paralyzed. But, then again, looking back on my life, both before and after my accident, I never would have thought *a lot* of things. How unpredictable life is and how quickly it changes. Add this one to the Lessons Learned the Hard Way column of life. Sure, deserts do receive rain, but witnessing it feels surreal, as if what is happening is out of place and just not supposed to happen. Compare the feeling to my reality: It rained in the desert on the one day that changed my life forever.

No one knew how long it would take for help to arrive. Meg told me soon after Matt left, in her calm, Ozzie-accented voice, "I don't know how long it will be, Joce. We could be here for a long time, really." Finally, far off in the distance, the wind carried the sound of a plane. Three and a half hours had passed since my accident occurred. Before mentally doing a dance of joy, my practicality kicked in. I did not muster too much excitement because no one knew what kind of plane it was. Given that nearby companies did scenic flights over the dunes, the plane could have been tourists as easily as the medical rescue team.

While Matt had gone to the campground for help, I had no idea "help" meant a plane. However, after getting a good look at it, Meg and Paula told me they saw a red cross on the bottom of the plane. Help had finally arrived. There I still lay with my face and body covered with wind blown, crusty sand. I completely trusted whatever people told me because I could not see for myself. Just after discovering that it was a medic plane, I heard the truck roar as Matt came speeding back to the accident site.

When help felt moments away, I started to feel pain. I eagerly listened to the plane circling. It flew over me once, twice, then again…ok, now I was getting irritated and wondered *what the fuck is taking so long??!! Just land the damn plane.* I had waited, very patiently, long enough. Without seeing the terrain around me, I had no idea that there were not any good straightaways on which to land the plane. The pilot flew over me a few times, scoping out the best and straightest landing spot close to me before he landed.

Once the plane was on the ground, the paramedics rushed over and quickly put an IV in me. To prepare me and talk me through the paramedics' activities, Sal said, "They are putting an IV in and you might get really cold." And I did. I had never had an IV before. Next came getting me on a stretcher. The paramedics had this metal stretcher that snapped apart in the middle. They gingerly rolled me to one side, while keeping my neck and back as immobile as possible, and tucked one side of the stretcher under me. Then just as carefully they rolled me the other way, put the other half under me and the two pieces clicked together. With all of this going on, I wanted to know who was taking care of me. With my eyes closed I asked, "What's your name?" He responded, "Oh, my name is Craig," sounding surprised at my inquiry. Even amidst the calamity and rushing around, I still wanted to know who helped me. With me immobilized and stable, the paramedics headed to the plane with me.

Rather than carrying me the distance to the plane, a tourist passing by had a little station wagon. A medic plane in the middle of the desert with a cluster of people gathered in a small area really draws a crowd. The medics concluded the vehicle would jostle me less than people carrying me on the stretcher so they put me on the bed of the wagon and very slowly drove me over to the plane. As they lifted me into the plane Ross said to me, "We'll see you in a few days, Joce." His voice conveyed encouragement, trying to remain upbeat about everything. However, I approach life realistically. I smiled and said, "No you won't, but thanks anyway." The diagnosis of my injuries awaited me at the hospital. People often ask me what was going through my mind, but, looking back, I wonder what was going through the minds of everyone else there.

The plane that rescued me.

Matt accompanied me on the plane to the hospital. Meg, the lead driver, needed to stay with the truck. Paula also wanted to come along, but the plane was too small. With the pilot, two paramedics, Matt, me and our rucksacks, there truly was no space for her. She decided to make her way up to Windhoek, Namibia's capital city (and where I was headed) the next day.

Once on the plane, Craig continued working on me. He said he wanted to administer some pain medicine. Now I felt much more pain and discomfort than at the dune, but nothing close to unbearable. However, before he started the medicine in my IV, he had to put a tube up through my nose, down my throat and into my stomach. This little procedure felt worse than breaking my back because I could feel *everything*. He said, "Open wide" and sprayed this stuff at the back of my throat to numb my gag reflex. Whatever that stuff was, it did not do shit to numb anything. All this time, I still could not see anything with my closed sand-encrusted eyes. I continued trusting everyone around me and did what they told me to do.

"The purpose of the tube", Craig said, "is if you throw up, it will come out of the tube and not up your throat which would cause you to choke." I wondered, *what would make me throw up?* My answer arrived quickly. Craig started the pain medicine and said, "Tell me when you start to feel nauseous." About five seconds later, I started feeling queasy and puked. Sure enough, it came right up and out of the tube as Craig predicted. These paramedics knew what they were doing. Finally, after completing everything else, Craig cleared the sand from my eyes. Immediately, hovering over me, I saw a young kid who resembled a blond, baby-faced Richie Cunningham from *Happy Days* doing all these medical procedures. Darting around the dark, cramped airplane, my eyes searched for Matt. Finding him tucked away in the rear left corner of the plane (not even three feet from me) our eyes locked. He looked very anxious.

At about 5:00 PM on April 13, I arrived at the hospital in Windhoek. Our group had been there about a week before my accident so the city was familiar. A little urban, metropolitan area with all the comforts of the West characterizes Windhoek. However, not knowing anything about the quality of the medical care system, given how Western the city appeared to be, I felt no qualms. While Matt appeared very freaked out, in comparison, I felt serene, as I had while waiting for the plane at the dune, which I do not think was a result from the pain medication. Later, my mother told me, "Jocelyn, the inner peace and calm you possessed was the Holy Spirit within you." I have come to believe that myself.

Through all this—what was I thinking? Nothing. Or nothing about what happened or what might be wrong. Questions did not frantically race through my mind. Not "I wonder what's wrong?" or "Will I ever walk again?" or "How badly am I hurt?" I was alive and thinking about the next thing—help coming, getting to the hospital, seeing the doctor, awaiting his diagnosis. But I did not think about the seriousness of the situation, what it really meant for me, for the rest of my life and the lives of those who knew me.

I was 26 years old.

"Two roads diverged in a wood, and I—
I took the one less traveled by,
And that has made all the difference."

—*The Road not Taken* by Robert Frost

Chapter Two
From There to Here

I survived a K through 12 Catholic school education—make of that what you will—and turned out just fine. The first public school I attended was the University of Michigan. My upbringing was rather conventional for the 1970's and 80's. No divorce, no family scandals, no dysfunction. A breadwinning dad, a mom who happily stayed home to raise their two daughters, then, when the girls started high school, went to work to help pay for college. How thankful I am for such a childhood. We were a good Catholic family that went to church every week and visited our relatives in the Detroit area for holidays and other family events. We relocated for my dad's job to Kalamazoo in western Michigan when I was in second grade and my sister was in fifth grade. Both my parents grew up in the Detroit area and we were the first from either side of the family to leave the east side of the state.

My sister, Gretchen, two years older, possessed many of the typical first child traits—more responsible, quieter, more reserved. I possessed more mischievous and daring qualities. Concealing myself in the center of the clothes racks while shopping so my mother could not find me; picking up still lit cigarette butts off the ground to try to smoke them—that did not last long; refusing to take naps at day care, but quietly looking at books instead while the other kids dozed. I was stubborn from a very early age. It drove my mother crazy at times. Around the ages of four or five, if she cut my sandwich straight down the middle instead of on a diagonal, I would refuse to eat it. She also had to

Gretchen and I in 1971

Me in 1973

fill my glass *exactly* halfway or I would not drink it. If I really did not want to do something, I did not. Conversely, if I really wanted to do something, I found a way to do it.

In between living in the Detroit area and Kalamazoo, we spent a few years in Toledo, Ohio. In Toledo I started kindergarten and attended most of second grade until we moved to Kalamazoo. We lived in a vibrant, eclectic neighborhood called the Old West End. Victorian houses lined the blocks. Our gold-colored house was almost 100 years old with both a front and a back staircase. Two stained glass windows decorated our living room. Leaded glass gave richness and stature to the TV room and the two gorgeous, thick wooden front doors.

The people in the neighborhood matched the uniqueness and vivacity of the houses. Many of the kids were the same age or within a few years of each other. We attended the Catholic elementary school nearby, St. Angela Hall. The parents jelled together just as easily as the kids. My friend Alison's dad, Paul, had a few nicknames for me. One was Miss Maude Hot Cycle and the other was Zsa Zsa G'Jocelyn (as in Zsa Zsa Gabor). I liked playing dress up a lot and could be a bit of an exhibitionist at times. We lived there a short time but made friends who have lasted a lifetime. Those were great years.

Moving was hard. I did not want to leave my friends and start a new school. But kids adapt and I made new friends in Kalamazoo. Yet we still kept in touch with the Toledo crowd. Even as young as 10 years old, I would take the five-hour Greyhound bus from Kalamazoo to Toledo by myself to visit my friends. Back then it was a much different world and safer to do such things. Today, taking the bus by oneself at that age would not be an option.

As I matured, I grew more reticent. It was not part of my nature to draw attention to myself as Zsa Zsa did at the age of five. In school, teachers liked me and I studied hard and earned good grades. Actually, my sister and I were very similar in that respect. We both worked hard to be good students and athletes. In our house, my parents emphasized academics and athletics rather than art or music. My parents trusted us, which came in very handy. In high school my parents would often go away for the weekend, thus leaving the house to me, as my sister already started college. No major parties occurred, but it gave my friends a place to go after going out to other parties.

I easily obtained the reputation as the responsible one among my friends' parents. Even today when my high school friends and I get together, it inevitably comes up that someone says, "I just told my mom I was going out with Jocelyn and she said, 'oh, that's okay then,'" as if my mere presence would protect their child from any harm or getting up to no good. In reality, that impression lacked accuracy, but it is what the parents believed. In the grand scheme of things and compared to what kids are like today, we were all good kids and never pushed the envelope too far. We went to parties and drank a little, but not uncontrollably, and we stayed out of trouble.

Given my upbringing, I followed the path my parents laid out for me—high school, college, then a job—the formula for success. All my friends followed the same path. It never occurred to me to do anything else. Possessing a very strong work ethic, I started babysitting at the age of 12 and helped my mother out during the summers when she ran LeDog, her hotdog cart, on the outdoor Kalamazoo Mall. At 16, my first real job was working at a TCBY where I continued until graduating from high school. Do not misunderstand me, I wanted to follow the college path. Leaving home to attend college sounded like a dream, freedom from the 'rents!! My narrow view from my sheltered upbringing did not provide me with the insight to question this "formula for success." Therefore in college, I expected the world to open up and reveal the mystery of what to do with my life (or so I naively thought). Of course I wanted to go!!!

My sister, two years older, but three grades ahead of me, attended the University of Michigan (U of M). After visiting her several times, I wanted to attend U of M as well. Go Blue! My graduating high school class had only 70 kids and about ten of us went to U of M. Half were part of my close knit group of friends, but once on campus most of us dispersed and went our separate ways. From my visits with Gretchen, I already knew my way round campus for the most part and loved Ann Arbor. Meeting my Resident Assistant at Stockwell, an all-girls dorm, for the first time, I told her I was a freshman. She looked shocked and said, "You're a freshman?" I hesitantly said, "Yeah. Why?" She replied, "most freshmen look scared and overwhelmed, but you don't." I suppose I found my element.

As a student, I dedicated much of my time to my studies in order to finish in four years. Starting college, I had not the slightest inkling about what to do with my life. At 18, how can anyone pick such a thing? It took over a year to commit to a major. The time came and I had to choose something. My reasoning for choosing English Literature over other possibilities? History—the wrong kind of reading, too many dates and facts; Psychology—everyone else was doing it; Economics or Political Science—(big yawn) need I say more? or Sociology—what kind of a job do you get with that degree? English won because I enjoyed reading and writing.

During my junior year enlightenment for a career finally arrived. I had an epiphany that Physical Therapy would be an ideal career. The wheels started turning as I considered changing my major to Physical Therapy or Sports Medicine. Because of my involvement with athletics and my interest in massage, I thought it might be a good fit. However, the wind in my sails quickly died when I discovered the requirements to change majors. Essentially, it meant starting from scratch with all science classes. Another four years of college stared me in the face. At the time, I only had a year and a half left. When selecting English, I purposely chose a path with NO math classes and very few credits of natural science. In high school, I took Calculus, Biology, Chemistry, Physics, so I knew all the fun I'd be missing. Being on track to finish in four years, I decided to stick with the original plan—English.

At the end of my junior year I hired on at the Real Seafood Company in downtown Ann Arbor as a waitress. Previous waitress experience came from summer jobs at a Denny's and a locally owned pizza restaurant in Kalamazoo. Real Seafood was in the upper echelon in terms of restaurant quality and clientele. By this time I called Ann Arbor home year round. Real Seafood became a part of my life. I kept the job throughout my senior year as well. I had carried 16 credits my first three years and could ease up a bit for my last year.

With my college years drawing to a close, I began to seriously consider what I would do after graduation. Aside from my short-lived desire to study Physical Therapy, I still had not solved the mystery of what to do with my life. I honestly could not think of any job I would rather do than my waiting job. The people, both my co-workers and the clientele, entertained me and I made a decent living. To celebrate my graduation, I bought myself a big present—a trip to Europe.

After graduating in May 1993, I embarked on my trip. When contemplating moving about the European countryside, I considered doing a Eurail Pass—a train pass that can be purchased for a set period of time and will take you throughout Europe by train. However, I would be traveling on my own. None of my friends could go with me due to jobs and plans for further education. Having never been to Europe and not knowing how big the language barrier might be, I was not too keen on the idea of riding on a train all over Europe by myself. Instead of scrapping my Europe idea because no one could go with me, I stopped in at a local travel agency to check out what organized trips existed and discovered a company called Contiki that specialized in trips for people 18 to 35 years old. I chose a six week trip through Europe. This trip would only happen once and I wanted to do it big.

I took a leave of absence from work with every intention

of returning to Ann Arbor and to the Real Seafood Company. In June 1993 I boarded a plane by myself in Detroit, flew into London, took the tube into the city to find my hotel and met my group at the hotel. Easy as pie, to me, anyway. I felt no fear or anxiety. I instead experienced excitement and anticipation for what the next six weeks held in store. My friends and family acted like doing this trip by myself was some monumental feat, but to me it seemed quite natural. I loved the feeling of adventure that came from this new path.

Once on the trip, the travel bug bit me, burrowed under my skin and intertwined itself with my body and soul. My eyes opened to a new world. On this fantastic trip, I was the lone American. Everyone else originated primarily from Canada, Oz or New Zealand. One of the first worldly lessons learned—those Kiwis (New Zealanders, the Kiwi is their national bird) and Ozzies can drink! Here was my chance to experiment and try loads of new things. I paid for the trip with my own money and felt no pressure from my parents or people I knew to behave in any particular way. Aside from celebrating my four years of hard work in college, the trip gave me a sense of free-spiritedness unlike anything else I had experienced up to that point in my life.

In the States, the University of Michigan carries a certain prestige and significance. To a busload of people not from the States, it meant I simply graduated from a university. And I liked it that way. I could sit down to chat with someone and the questions "what do you do?" or "what was your major?" would never come up. We all were traveling to hang out, see the sights and have a good time. In Europe I adopted the motto "you're here for a good time, not a long time." Things like getting enough sleep could be done later, too many fun things to do with so little time.

It excited me to be with so many people from other countries who had left their homes to explore the world. The thrill and excitement of it all was infectious and compelled me to do more traveling. I realized how few Americans do extensive travel for long periods of time. I also discovered my naïveté when it came to world traveling. When booking my airline tickets, I flew into London the day before the trip started and I flew out the day after it ended. It did not even occur to me to stay an extra week in England to see some of the sights round London, as many other people on the trip planned to do.

Many of the people from Oz and New Zealand remained in England on work visas. I learned the beauty of being part of the Commonwealth, of which the U.S. is not. If you have citizenship from a Commonwealth country (such as England, Canada, Australia and New Zealand) and are in your twenties it is easy to get work visas for other Commonwealth countries. However, if one is from the U.S. a work visa for a Commonwealth country is damn near impossible to obtain. Others simply took a year off from their daily life to travel around the world. How many Americans do you know who do this? Yes, we study abroad for a semester or two and take a holiday here and there. But our culture, with its 40-hour plus work week and two weeks holiday time each year, does not foster extended travel.

I hated saying goodbye to the great friends I met, but

knew I would keep in touch with some of them. Once back in Ann Arbor, reality crept back into my life. Life began to lose the sparkle I discovered in Europe. What was I going to do with my life?? Additionally, life back in Kzoo with my parents and family turned tumultuous. The devoted, closely knit family I had only four years ago, no longer existed. My family's metamorphosis had actually begun during my sophomore year in college.

One October evening during my fall sophomore semester, I received a call from my parents. They told me they put our house, the house Gretchen and I grew up in, on the market and were purchasing a new house in Kalamazoo. While not uncommon for parents to move after their children leave the house, it shocked me because my parents had never discussed wanting to move. The house sold quickly and by Thanksgiving Mom and Dad had moved into their new home. I never even got the chance to go through the old house one last time.

On my first visit back to Kzoo that year at Thanksgiving, I went "home" to the unfamiliar new house. Aside from it not being my home, I did not like the house. From the outside, it looked well-built and contemporary. The inside did not emit a good vibe. The house possessed some unique features like a loft suite for the master bedroom, a wood-burning stove and a beautiful sun room, but the poorly lit interior and lack of windows in the front cast an indescribable chill over the house. What drew my parents to it? Dad liked the modern design of the secluded house and Mom only wanted to do what made him happy.

Over the next three years, my family drastically changed.

First the new house, then Dad desired more space not only in his home, but also in his marriage. Dad said he craved the opportunity to live completely on his own, something he had never done. My mother loved him dearly. In an attempt to keep him happy and the family together, she agreed to his moving into his own apartment for a while. Every constant and everything stable I had known changed suddenly.

My dad also stopped going to Mass. I am a cradle Catholic, as were my parents, and their parents. Even though raised Catholic, college life offered me a new-found freedom. No one nagged me about attending church each week, so I did not go. During my sophomore year, Dad became more interested in Eastern religions and decided he did not want to go to church anymore. Because she wanted to support him and his decision, my mother stopped attending as well. Another significant change was that my dad started psychotherapy and taking Prozac for depression. All of these things are typically good to get someone mentally healthy, but with my dad, we were not seeing any positive benefits. When my maternal grandmother passed away, I remember Dad taking me back to Ann Arbor from Detroit after the funeral. Driving down the road, Dad turned to me and said, "Would you still love me if I divorced your mother?"

** ** ** ** ** **

Even though all this happened in Kzoo and was about my parents' marriage, it still heavily involved my sister and me. This was my life, my family as I had known it for the past 20 years. My sister was more affected because she lived in Kzoo. Seeing my mother and father more often, running into friends of the family on the street or at the mall, people knowing that our parents were not together or, even worse, people not knowing and asking my sister, "How are your parents?" While greatly impacting each of our lives, it played a bigger part in her day-to-day life than in mine.

The year after returning from Europe, I existed in limbo, not knowing what to do. My life consisted of showing up at the restaurant by 10 or 10:30 A.M. to work lunch, then dinner (with maybe a short break in between) until at least 9:00. If it was later in the week I would stop by the bar after work, have a drink, play some darts or shoot pool, then head home and get up to work the lunch shift the next day. A rather hamster-wheel like existence.

Luckily I lived far from the restaurant and drove to work everyday. I say "luckily" because it prevented me from getting as pissed as some of my coworkers and squandering my night's tips at the bar. I felt a responsibility to remain sober when driving a car. My Real Seafood days were fun and I forged friendships that remain intact today. I am so thankful for the chance to have met so many colorful, eccentric and endearing characters, both co-workers and customers.

I stayed in close contact with a few people from my European holiday, one of whom was Andrea (Andy) from Toronto. She had one year to finish at university and decided she wanted to take an extended trip after graduation. Andy phoned me one evening in late 1993 and said, "My friend, Barb, and I decided to spend a year in Australia and New

Zealand. Do you want to go? We are looking at leaving in the fall of 1994." With no particular career path in sight and not even close to picking one, I jumped at the chance. In the subsequent months, I busted my ass working double shifts at the restaurant to save as much money as possible. I had the vigor of youth and a goal in sight to pull me through those long hard days. In October of 1994, the three of us left from Toronto.

During this time, my parents were trying to work things out. To see me off, they both drove me to the Toronto airport. Being at an airport again, ready to experience a different world, filled me with enthusiasm. Because of Canadian airport security standards, my parents could only accompany me to the security checkpoint. I expected them to come with me to the gate. The time came, more quickly than I anticipated, to say goodbye to them. Reality suddenly slapped me in the face. I thought *I will not see them for a year! I will not hug them, see them or speak to them face-to-face, oh, I will miss them!* My eyes welled up as I hugged and kissed them goodbye. Queuing up in the security line, I gave them one more glance and a tearful wave. They waved back and walked back through the airport. But as I boarded the plane, settled into my seat and felt the freedom of the plane leaving the ground, the sadness quickly faded. I had the first stop of our trip to look forward to— meeting Barb and Andy in Honolulu during a layover. We had purchased our airline tickets separately for the trip. Their route to New Zealand included an extra stop in Vancouver before reaching Honolulu.

After boarding the same plane in Honolulu, we hit New

Zealand for a six-week trip of the North and South Islands. We booked transportation with a tour group called Kiwi Experience. What a blast! We got on the Experience bus in Auckland on the North Island and were to fly out of Christ Church on the South Island in December to go over to Australia. What made the Experience great was the flexibility to get on and off the bus as you liked. Kiwi Experience did not plan the trip for you, it merely transported you from town to town. If we liked a certain area, we could stay there as long as we liked. We often ran into the same people in different cities but also met a whole new group with each bus trip.

To this day, New Zealand is, by far, my favorite country. The people there are magnificent. I found their philosophy of life a refreshing change from the American way of life. They make time for more leisure. Their friendliness and hospitality surpasses that of anywhere else I have ever been. They possess openness and kindness that I had never before encountered in complete strangers. The breathtaking scenery mesmerized me and drew me close. Watch the Lord of the Rings movies (filmed in New Zealand) and you will experience some of the beauty. Plus, I met some amazing travelers and reunited with friends along the way. One great thing about my European Conitki trip was meeting all the people from New Zealand and Oz whom I could now visit when passing through their towns. I experienced true hospitality, and people always wanted to show us a good time.

If you crave an adrenaline rush, New Zealand will satisfy the craving. Anything fun, wild and crazy—you can do it in

New Zealand. I went bungee jumping, tandem skydiving, caving, rappelling down cliffs, jet boating, swimming with dolphins, mountain biking and hiking. I learned that waterfalls and mountains made my soul soar far more than a beach. Whatever your fancy, New Zealand has it all!

Unlike American culture, New Zealand has a no-fault personal injury system in place for anyone living in or visiting the country. If one is injured at work or at play, the government will take care of medical costs and other expenses without placing blame on any party. Because the government takes care of such costs, the injured person is not allowed to sue for personal injury compensation. A far cry from the "litigation happy" culture perpetuated in the U.S.

While there I met Peter who was traveling with his mates. Scottish, enchanting, sexy, lovely Peter. Given enough time in the same location, we would have had one of the most passionate affairs of my life. We met on a Kiwi Experience bus trip on the South Island. He sat behind me. I introduced myself as Lady J (the nickname my friends bestowed upon me). He possessed a needling sense of humor and started calling me Miss G, just to bug me. For the first time in my life, I experienced pure chemistry with someone. We were drawn to each other. Having recently finished college, the guys I hung around were just that, guys. Peter was a man at 31, with me being 23 soon to turn 24. And I do not know where those Scottish boys learn how to kiss, but holy shit! They could teach American boys a thing or two. I have never experienced anyone quite like him again. Not only did I hang out with him in New Zealand, but had the opportunity to see him in Sydney, then in Perth in Western Australia a few months later. Over time we lost touch.

I celebrated my twenty fourth birthday in Queenstown, New Zealand and it was my best birthday ever. We had a fun night out and my friends gave me a fish hook bone carving, a popular Maori carving worn on a string or chain around the neck. Maoris are the indigenous inhabitants of New Zealand. Each hook carving signifies things like wealth, power or good fortune. The one given to me signified good luck and good fortune. The carving has to be given as a gift to you or it brings the opposite of what it signifies. Once I placed it around my neck, it rarely came off. People ask, "Were you wearing it when you had your accident?" Yes, I was, and to this day, I wear a fish hook carving from New Zealand around my neck

After the quick jaunt around New Zealand, Andy, Barb and I arrived in Australia in December 1994, very close to the

Queenstown, New Zealand on my 24ᵗʰ birthday, 1994

holidays. How very peculiar seeing decorated Christmas trees when it was 80 degrees outside. We flew into Melbourne, went down to Tasmania, then headed up to Sydney, got a flat there and tried to find some work. Andy found a waitressing job. Barb and I did some odd jobs, but nothing steady. I left Sydney first to start up the coast to Cairns, then head over to Western Australia. Barb and Andy headed north as well, but were traveling back to Canada through the Far East and would not be following my same path. We traveled together for about four and a half months, then I took off on my own. I felt no nervousness or fear. Having met so many fantastic people along the way thus far, I knew I would meet more.

When coming out of Sydney, I met up with three Brits who had just met each other as well—Davina, Jon and Mark. We signed up for a weekend trip to an island made entirely of sand called Fraser Island, where we rented a four-wheel-

In Australia at the iconic Sydney Opera House, 1995

Hiking in King's Canyon, Australia in 1995

drive truck. Then we camped and drove all over the island. Once back on the mainland and in Airlie beach, the four of us enrolled in a scuba class to be certified on the Great Barrier Reef. People coming down from the north advised us to get certified somewhere south of Cairns. Cairns is a popular tourist destination on the east coast of northern Australia. Large segments of the reef in Cairns are dead and gray from too many divers and snorkelers touching and standing on the reef, which instructors implore people not to do. When I arrived in Cairns I did go diving to make the comparison. My dive experience farther south in Airlie Beach let me glimpse an unquestionably more healthy and vibrant part of the Great Barrier Reef. As part of the class we stayed on a boat for three days to complete open water dives. What a thrill to experience a whole other world beneath the water's surface. After finishing the course we booked beds at a backpacker (hostel) in Airlie Beach. I decided to phone my parents since I had not spoken to them in a while.

This particular backpacker had a number of cabins with multiple bunks in each. Walking through the grounds up to the phones, I thought only of my amazing scuba diving experience. No one in my family had ever done something like this! An entire world mostly unseen to us on land existed below the water's surface. I could not wait to tell my parents. By this time, my dad had moved back home, and I recounted the details of my diving with both parents listening on different phones in the house. However, even though thousands of miles away, I felt tension and strain in their voices. Finally, Dad said, "We're getting a divorce."

I was stunned. I shuffled back to our cabin in a daze. Jon greeted me at the door and I blurted out, "My parents are getting divorced," and started crying. Not knowing how to deal with a crisis and being English, Jon said, "Do you want a cuppa tea, luv?" I just laughed and he sat me down on one of the bunks.

Even though I heard the words, the magnitude of their meaning did not fully register. I was so far away that had I managed to tune my family's disintegration out of my everyday life. I traveled on, having a good time.

After I left Cairns, I headed for Ayers Rock. I did a two-day tour to visit Ayers Rock, then proceeded to Western Australia by plane to see my friend Penny—another European trip connection.

Penny's family owned a plant nursery in Perth. I stayed with her for two months and worked in the nursery. It ranks as one of my best jobs ever. I loved the caretaking, the nurturing, the dirtiness, plus I got to drive a tractor. And, in getting the plants ready for retail, I fulfilled the lifelong childhood dream of using a price gun. When at the grocery store with my mom, I would marvel with a slight twinge of envy as the stock boy would slap prices on items with lightening speed. Ker-chunk, ker-chunk, ker-chunk went the price gun. I would think *what a lucky duck, I want to do that someday.* Thank God I eventually became more ambitious.

In May 1995 I headed back to New Zealand. I knew I would stay for at least three months, which is the duration of a tourist visa. I found my way to Taupo, a city on the North Island, landed a job cleaning at a hostel called The Rainbow

Lodge to receive free board and waited tables at a café in town. For the next few months, I hung out and had plenty to do. It was a stress-free life. Before leaving New Zealand, I did journey back down to the South Island to swim with dolphins in Kaikoura; an utterly amazing experience. The frigid water required wearing full wet suits with booties, gloves and head coverings. The boat found a pod of dolphins and everyone jumped in. Once my breathing regulated from the shock of the freezing water, the dolphins came into view. I floated in the water surrounded by dolphins merely an arm's length away.

In early November 1995, I arrived back in Kalamazoo. Since the big announcement of the divorce, Dad had moved out, then back in, and was living there when I returned. However, he did not stay long. I remember that Christmas well because it marked the last Christmas we shared together as a single family. My family, my security, my foundation and what I had known as reality for 25 years changed. I remember most vividly the gift my mother gave to my father—a set of luggage. How ironic. After Christmas he moved out, for good.

In order to make the process as cordial as possible, my mother agreed to a fairly amicable divorce. Then came the phone call from my dad's co-worker revealing that he had been having an affair. This changed everything. My mother retained an attorney who would protect and fight for her. As the divorce negotiations wore on, lots of astounding information surfaced. The woman my dad was seeing had also been married and was breaking up her marriage as well.

She had two boys that my dad treated like sons—they actually went to the same Catholic high school as Gretchen and I had. When I went to New Zealand and Australia I kept my car. The car belonged to my Grandpa Dettloff, who would give my sister and me his old cars, and my parents paid the insurance on it. While I was overseas, Dad told Mom that he would keep the car at his apartment and use it from time to time to keep it running. In reality his girlfriend's 17- year-old son drove the car the entire time. Unbeknownst to her, my mother kept paying the insurance on it. That did not sit too well with me. Dad returned the car after I got back from New Zealand.

Within just a few years, our closely knit, loving family disintegrated. After 32 years of marriage, my parents' divorce became final in January 1997. Divorce is not easy for children at any age. At 26 years old, I felt devastated. Family and friends could not believe what happened. It seemed like a bad dream and I wanted to wake up so it would end. In all the years of knowing my father, I never thought him capable of doing the things he did. People get divorced often but do not engage in such reckless, destructive behavior. As we came to learn, this affair was not his first one.

For the longest time, neither my sister nor I spoke to Dad. With my being open-minded and free-spirited, I think he thought I would be less judgmental and more accepting than my sister. We still loved him but were furious with him. And anger management is not something we were taught as children. Over the years I learned to let a lot go because hanging on to the anger, the hurt and negative energy does not nurture my well being. To be angry takes so much more energy than letting go and being at peace. Things will never be the way they once were between us, but I love him and he will always be my dad.

In November of 1995, for the Christmas season, I worked as a gift wrapper at a high end gift shop in downtown Kalamazoo. Like working at the nursery in Australia, this was another fabulous job. I loved the gorgeous thick paper and beautiful bows and ribbons in so many colors. The gift wrapping station was located in the back storage area so I could wear jeans to work and did not have to interact with customers on the floor. After the holiday rush, the job ended and I took on a receptionist job during the day and tended bar evening and weekends at an Applebee's. I remained directionless in terms of a career path. I did know that I did not want to stay in Kalamazoo for too long. I lived at home with Mom and did not pay rent; thus I started saving money for my next trip.

In 1996 I started thinking about my next travel destination. A fellow American, whom I had met while in New Zealand, raved about visiting Africa. He went with a British company called Dragoman and said they were top notch. Given that Africa was rustic, third-world and potentially dangerous, I decided to investigate organized trips rather than try to get around on my own. I planned on spending three months in Africa and then going to the west coast of Ireland for another three months where a friend from high school, Mary, had been living. She would be able to help me find a job and a place to live.

I scoped out a few companies that ran what were called overland trips. Dragoman conducted such trips all over the world, even here in the United States. On an overland trip the truck provides all the camping and cooking equipment and travelers only need to bring a sleeping bag, clothes and a roll mat for sleeping. Travelers primarily stay in campgrounds or sometimes bush camp, depending on the location. This would certainly be different from my other travels. I signed up for two six-week segments. Little did I know how truly life-changing this trip would be.

Close to my departure date, one evening when working at Applebee's, this guy came up to the bar and placed a takeout order. We made small talk and I told him my plans to travel to Africa and Ireland. I went on to explain that I was not on the typical career mill that others jumped on after college, partly from not knowing what I wanted to do, partly from wanting to see what the rest of the world had to offer. When he got up to leave, he firmly grasped my hand, wished me luck, looked me straight in the eye and said, "You're doing the right thing."

Like the Contiki trip in Europe, I had no idea who would be my traveling companions. I left from Chicago O'Hare, flew to England for a few days to see some friends, then flew down to Nairobi, Kenya to meet up with people that I would be with for the next three months.

Witnessing people survive with so little impacted me the most. Here in the States people whine when the cable goes out or hate having to stand in a long line at the abundantly stocked grocery store. It altered my perspective on things.

Driving through little villages delighted and surprised me. When the children heard the roar of the truck in the distance they came running out from everywhere just to wave at us. As the truck lumbered through, the children jumped, waved and smiled. We waved and smiled back. The first time this happened, I realized the far reach of American culture. Here we are in the middle of rural, vast Africa, and one of the children running out to us is wearing a red Chicago Bulls T-shirt.

The markets, with locals trying to sell art and other local trinkets, opened my eyes. I wanted to buy something from a vendor and he wanted me to pay with my black Teva sandals. Now, I paid good money for those back in the States and was not about to give them up. I said to him, "If I give you my shoes, what will I wear?" He replied, "You are rich, you go home, you buy more." By U.S. standards, I was far from rich; however, the mere fact that I was there signified to him I had money. My sandals remained on my feet.

The first segment of the trip ended in Harare, Zimbabwe, where the second segment began. On the way to Harare, we stopped to see Victoria Falls in Zambia, then crossed over a bridge into Zimbabwe to the city of Victoria Falls. The falls on the Zambian side were breathtakingly majestic. I had an opportunity to take the plunge and bungee jump for the second time in my life. This time from the tallest natural bungee in the world—111 meters (333 feet)! Once in Vic Falls for a few days, I decided to check out the falls from the Zim side, just to compare. For the record, the Zambian wins. I took off from the campground on my own for the short walk to the falls. While there, an afternoon shower rolled in, so I headed back. The shower did not last long, but when it started, people ran for shelter leaving the streets deserted. I strolled along carrying my sunglasses and camera in a plastic bag, swinging it to and fro. I passed two local teenage boys. As they passed me, one of them snatched the bag right out of my hand and bolted. Instinct kicked in. I turned and ran after him—*I ran track in high school,* I thought, *I can catch him.* When he saw me chasing him, and gaining, he dropped the bag and continued running. All I could think about was, *oh, no, my camera with all those pictures on it.* I wanted it back.

"We lead our lives like water flowing down a hill, going more or less in one direction until we splash into something that forces us to find a new course."

—*Memoirs of a Geisha* by Arthur Golden

CHAPTER THREE
A NEW REALITY

At the hospital, the paramedics hoisted me onto a gurney, snapped apart the metal frame, removed it from underneath me and rushed me into the emergency room. I noticed Matt at my side at first, then he vanished. He left to take care of registration, insurance information and those details. Prior to starting the trip, the drivers record and keep all contact and insurance information from everyone on the truck for situations just like this.

When the doctor entered the room, Matt had returned. The doctor looked to be in his thirties. He sported a short trimmed beard and resembled George Michael (very attractive). He did not look like a doctor—as in no white coat or stethoscope around his neck. He proffered no introduction as he peered down at me, flicking encrusted sand off my skin with a look of almost disdain. In silence, I waited for him to say something. "I want you to know you'll probably never walk again," were the very first words he spoke. Flat out. No, "Hi, how are you doing? I'm Dr. Schroeder, we're going to take care of you now." No small talk or words of comfort, just the facts, blunt and to the point. Matt's confidence level in the doctor plummeted at his atrocious bedside manner. Matt commented later, "I cannot believe what an unfeeling twat the doctor was."

Despite the slap-in-the-face, shocking dose of reality from

the doctor, directness has its benefits. People often ask, "How did you react?" Although it sounds nearly implausible, I just said, "OK." Dr. Schroeder's words did not pierce my ears like fingernails on a chalk board. I did not cringe or writhe in pain and agony when hearing, "you'll probably never walk again." And the pain meds cannot be credited for my rather tranquil reaction. By then, I had already been paralyzed for a few hours. Nothing changed and no feeling returned. What else was I going to do at that point? How would any extreme emotional reaction help the situation? The time spent at the bottom of the sand dune had provided time for my new reality to sink in and take hold.

After Dr. Schroeder dropped the bomb, the nurses went to work cutting off my clothes and scraping off sand. Seeing my favorite pair of navy soccer shorts cut apart bummed me out more than being paralyzed. Here I was paralyzed, thousands of miles from home and I am concerned about ruining my shorts—silly, huh? Aren't we funny sometimes? At this point, Matt disappeared again to tend to more insurance details. With my sandy clothes finally discarded in a pile on the floor, Dr. Schroeder informed me I would have an MRI done immediately to take pictures of my back.

I had never had an MRI done. I do not know how long it all took. I remember lying very still in a huge metal cocoon while this machine loudly churned around me. The technician spoke to me through a microphone, "OK, lie very still." Not too difficult with my body 75 percent paralyzed. They took various pictures. Some "shots" took over a minute, others took only 30 seconds. No wonder claustrophobic people experience anxiety when getting CAT scans and MRI's. Dr. Schroeder made no comment to me about the scans or what he thought may have happened. In the hall, out of my earshot, he revealed to Matt the real deal. "It looks like she has broken some vertebrae. She is lucky to be alive." On some level I knew this without being told, even when lying at the bottom of the sand dune. Intuitively, I did not sense this condition would be temporary or that things would be better in the morning.

At about 8:00 P.M., they finally brought me into ICU and hooked me up to all sorts of machines. An IV, an oxygen pulse monitor on my finger, plus that lovely tube still up my nose. The doctor must have known that the rest of my bones remained intact because he took no additional X-rays. The nurses in ICU closely watched the monitors for any other internal injuries or bleeding. The next 24 to 48 hours remained critical in stabilizing my system.

Despite paralysis, the numb portions of my body still possessed a certain "feeling" kind of like the prickle of a leg that fell asleep, but much more dull. The numbness started at chest level. With curiosity and trepidation, I slowly moved my hands down my body. Starting where I had feeling I inched my hands down my torso to my hips, extending my arms as far as I could with my head and neck immobilized. My hands felt my trunk, but my trunk could not sense the touch of my hands. My torso and stomach felt swollen with an almost hollow sensation. Have you ever taken a CPR class or felt one of those rubber/plastic dummies used for instruction? My body felt like one of those dummies, very thick and dead.

Tapping my fingers against my ribcage and stomach, I almost expected to hear a deep, empty thud. However, this was not some foreign object separate from my body, it was my body.

When Matt stepped out to tend to registration, he phoned my insurance company to notify them of what happened. For starters, the insurance rep had no idea Namibia existed, let alone its location. The rep began launching a series of questions at Matt because the rep thought Matt had to be making this up. With the anxiety and all that occurred that day, Matt had had enough of the insurance company. He hung up and phoned Dragoman in England to let them take the reins on this one. Since I had insurance, the medics took me to a private hospital, the MediClinic in Windhoek, and not a government public hospital. And as a result, I most likely received better care. As I found out later, Dr. Schroeder was German and did his medical training in South Africa. He also held the position of the spinal trauma specialist for the American Peace Corps. I was being well looked after.

Judy headed the nursing team in ICU. She was a tall, slender, cheerful woman with short black hair. She greeted me with her South African accent and helped me get settled in ICU. Matt stayed with me until about 11:00 P.M., when the nurses told him he needed to leave. He made sure I was OK, then slipped out and booked a room at a Bed & Breakfast just a few doors down from the hospital. I felt no anxiety about his leaving. I knew he would return the next morning. Though I was exhausted from the day's events, sleep did not come easily that first night, if at all. Simply too many blips and bleeps from those damn machines around me.

The next day Matt arrived early, still looking very stressed out. Since he smoked, I asked him, "Have you had a cigarette yet?" He replied, "I've had seven." It was only 8 or 9 in the morning. With a broken back and unstable spine, movement of my head, neck and body was prohibited. As such, the nurses could not do much to remove the sand still on me or encrusted in my hair. Six months to a year or more after my accident, while cleaning my ears with a Q-tip, a grain of sand would come out on occasion. Remnants of the Namib desert and Sossusvlei might be ingrained in me for the rest of my life.

It was now Monday morning, nearly 24 hours of paralysis. My mental state and coping mechanisms remained unchanged. My spirits were up as I looked forward to Paula leaving the truck and making her way back to Windhoek to join us at the hospital. Relatively early in the day, the phone calls started. Many people from the States called to check on me. Mom, Gretch, Dad and other friends. Word of what happened traveled fast amongst my various social circles. The unexpected phone calls surprised me. I was half way 'round the world, before the dirt cheap international calling rates that exist today. Just after finding out about the accident, Mom started calling everyone to ask them to start praying for me. Judy, the nurse, said, "You are getting more calls than a call girl." For the first time I completely understood how having visitors at the hospital can be exhausting. By the afternoon, even with only talking on the phone, I was spent.

Mom, and others, were relieved just to hear my voice and know that I sounded fine. We all have our own expectations of how a newly paralyzed person might sound—depressed, groggy, distressed, drained. But I did not sound any of those. Maybe a bit tired, but I sounded like, well, like me. As if I were casually lounging on the bed wrapped up in conversation rather than lying there paralyzed, unable to walk. I explained to Mom that the doctor was waiting for my system to stabilize before doing surgery. She told me right away, "I'm coming to Namibia as soon as I can get on a plane."

The accident occurred on Sunday. She wanted to be on a plane by Monday or Tuesday, but had to wait a few extra days due to not having a valid passport. Friends from Kalamazoo drove her three hours to Chicago to apply in person and immediately receive a passport. This was pre 9/11 and I wonder if she or anyone else would receive a passport so quickly today. Although it is starting to change, very few Americans have passports. I advise parents to obtain passports if they have children who travel overseas. To hop on a plane at a moment's notice may be critical in an emergency situation. No matter how urgent or serious a situation may be, if you need to go overseas and do not have a passport, you ain't goin' nowhere.

Having Matt and Paula there comforted me. They were truly a blessing. Throughout the ordeal, people surrounded me. I did not spend much time by myself, unless I wanted to. I remember meeting Paula the first day of the trip. I climbed aboard the truck and she stood in the back, glanced at me and said, "You look just like Jodie Foster." I smiled and asked her name. She said, "Paula." I asked her three times to say her name. Not to be a smart ass, but she was from England

and it sounded to me like she was saying Pola, as in cola. Finally it clicked and I blurted out with my suave American accent, "Oh, PAULA!!" We laughed. She had fun trying to say different things with an American accent like "parking lot." The English call them car parks.

Matt and Paula spent loads of time with me. I never lost my sense of humor and neither did they. We still chatted about people on the truck and about places we visited, mixed in with doctor stopping by, phone calls and questions to see if I needed anything. They did not exhibit any apprehension even if they were freaking out on the inside. This was my first inkling that the better I handled my accident, the more normal and ordinary people acted around me. I did not want them to feel uncomfortable. Matt spent most of the time sitting next to me holding my hand. Matt is not a guy of many words. His hand holding and even the silence exhibited more emotion than he would have ever been able to express to me in words.

On Tuesday, Dr. Schroeder waltzed in with the results of my MRI. He held them up to the light and showed me my broken back. Aside from the broken vertebrae and spinal cord damage, I did not have any other serious injuries, no other broken bones or internal organ damage or bleeding. I studied the films from my immobilized position and asked, "Based on these, do you think my spinal cord severed?" Silently he closed his eyes and nodded his head. Looking up at his face, I acceptingly said, "Okay." How would any of the more extreme reactions—crying, anger, unbelief, shouting—help my situation? It was no attempt to "be brave" in front of my friends or the doctor. Instinctively my coping mechanisms kicked in.

In asking him more questions about my break, he explained, "You broke your back at the Thoracic 5 vertebrae," which at the time meant nothing to me. I only knew I could not feel or move most of my body. Since then, I have come to learn (and learn very well) I acquired a Thoracic 5 (T-5) complete spinal cord injury. Spinal cord injuries are divided into two main categories—complete and incomplete. Complete means there is no feeling or movement from the point of injury down. Incomplete indicates some nerve pathways remain intact and people still have some movement and/or feeling. Those with incomplete injuries may still have the ability to stand and/or walk. Within the complete and incomplete categories, most individuals are either paraplegics (paras) with two limbs affected or quadriplegics (quads) with four limbs affected. Affected does not mean total loss of function. When people hear "quad" they usually assume someone is like Christopher Reeve, who could not move at all and for a while needed a ventilator to breathe.

Realistically, quads can be highly functional, to the point that it might not be apparent that he/she is a quad. It all depends on the level of injury. The spine divides into three areas, the Cervical region, which is the neck (C1-7), the Thoracic region, which is the chest and torso (T-1-12), and the Lumbar region, which is the lower back (L1-4). Christopher Reeve broke his neck at C1-C2, the highest point at which the neck can break. Someone breaking his neck at C7 is *almost* a para in that he has arm and tricep function, but does not have full hand function and strength. For example, he may be able to pick up a bottle, but not able to grip and twist off the cap.

Try this, where you are sitting right now, if you are able, put your hands down on each side of you, press down and lift yourself. You just experienced the use of the triceps muscle. With a break at the C7/C6 level, the triceps still function. A level or two higher, like C5, the biceps function, but not the triceps. Without the triceps muscle, one cannot lift or move oneself around. The precarious thing about neck injuries is all the nerves to the hands and arms run through the neck. One level or two higher could mean a world of difference in what one can and cannot do. For example, a C7 injury can live completely independently and not need assistance with transfers or personal care. With a higher injury, the person may need help with dressing, cooking, transfers and all personal care.

Moving down to the Thoracic region, the torso area, a level or two does not make that much difference. For me, a T5 complete injury means I do not have one iota of trunk or abdominal muscle that works to support and hold me upright. At the T5 level, nerve connection to those muscles has been lost so they no longer contract and function to support me. Mind you, I do sit up straight because I lean against something behind me like the backrest on my wheelchair or use my arms to remain upright if nothing is behind me to lean against. My lateral muscles provide some support in side to side motion because their "staring point" is above T5. All the muscle fibers are connected so if the upper part of the muscle develops, the lower portion will as well, even if it is below the point of injury. When seeing a para, or someone using a wheelchair who can also use his/her arms and hands, people generally assume the person is paralyzed from the waist down. In my case I am paralyzed from the chest down. My paralysis stops and starts at my bra line. I have what I call my fade zone, a short area in which moving down my torso I have full feeling, then dull feeling, then nothing. With a T6 or T7 injury, I may have gained use of my upper abs and with development by sheer attachment, some lower abs. The lower the Thoracic injury, the more trunk support and stability the person possesses. Although I did not fully comprehend the ramifications of a T5 injury, I recognized that fully functional arms and hands were a blessing.

With injuries to the Lumbar region, the person retains full trunk support. Not all, but most of those I have met with Lumbar injuries can move some leg muscles and in some cases even stand and take a few steps if hanging on to something.

** ** ** ** ** **

To help pass the time, the nurses scored us a TV and VCR to watch movies. On Wednesday, Matt and Paula visited the video store and returned with *Casino* and *Dumb and Dumber*. I had already seen both movies and liked them. Part of me hates to admit it, but *Dumb and Dumber* is hilarious. I knew we would have a good laugh watching it. I still could not move or prop up my head, so tackling this obstacle became the next priority. Having seen this situation before, the nurses rigged up a mirror viewing system. The nurses placed a mirror on wheels over me, then tilted it so I could see the TV. Brilliant! At this point it had been months since I watched TV or a movie.

Gazing up into the mirror for the first time since the accident, horror washed over me. It never occurred to me that I should ask to see a mirror. While I sustained no additional internal injuries, everyone failed to mention the massive black eye covering nearly the entire right side of my face. Maybe they assumed my broken back was enough and did not want to add to my delicate emotional state by telling me how bad my face looked. My face did not hurt so that provided no indication of the injury. My guess is when I hit the mound of dirt at the bottom of the dune, my hand flew up and hit my face. Thankfully with only temporary bruising.

We did have a good time watching the movies. *Dumb and Dumber* was just as funny as the first time I saw it. We all were laughing, and while laughter is the best medicine, I tried not to laugh too hard, because it hurt.

On Thursday, the small, three-bed ICU needed my bed for a more serious injury coming in. At this point I knew my surgery would take place on Friday. Before leaving the hospital and flying home, my spine needed to be fused and stabilized. They moved me into a room with another American girl. Coincidentally, within a day of my accident, there had been a truck accident with another overland company. The driver was changing tapes in the tape deck, swerved, skidded off the road and rolled. One or two people on the truck died. This

American girl was from around Baltimore, certainly from the East coast—accent and all. The hospital staff assumed that two people from the same country would make fine roommates.

"The Miserable Cow" is the nickname Matt and Paula cooked up for her. Although we shared a room, I have no idea what she looked like. With our injuries, neither of us could get up out of bed and since my spine was not yet stabilized, I could not even turn my head. In the accident, she had broken her pelvis, which would eventually heal. Here I am with a broken back, paralyzed, will most likely never walk again, and she is irritated and bitching to me because she will have to be off work for six to eight weeks once she gets home. Not to diminish how her accident affected her life, but I really could not conjure up much (if any) sympathy for her. However, she did not have anyone with her to help her sort out any details about medical care, insurance or getting home. She had to do that all on her own.

Later on Thursday afternoon, my breathing turned shallow and rapid. Matt and Paula had been out for a while and were a bit alarmed to return and discover my difficulty breathing. Dr. Schroeder was not at the hospital, so the nurses strapped an oxygen mask on me to see if that would help. I tried to take a nap, but could not. Still my laborious breathing continued. Finally my doctor called and instructed the nurses to give me Valium to calm me down. He said I was probably anxious about the surgery taking place the next day (this is what Matt and Paula told me). I remember Paula placing the pill in my mouth, swallowing it and her telling me, "It will calm you down." In a weary, breathy voice I replied, "But I'm not excited." I admit, sometimes the doctor does know best—after taking the Valium, my breathing went back to normal and I was able to sleep.

That evening, nurses moved me back into ICU to prep me for surgery. Or maybe they realized I needed closer monitoring. The next day was Friday, April 18, not only the day for my surgery, but also the day for my mother's arrival—and her birthday.

Preparation for surgery began early Friday morning. Dr. Schroeder and the surgeon, Dr. Opitz, came to talk with me. While not the key performer, Dr. Schroeder would assist Dr. Opitz. Dr. Opitz was a very tall, imposing, German-looking man with a coarse mustache and gray/blonde hair. While he looked more intimidating than Dr. Schroeder, he greeted me warmly with a handshake and smile. He explained what would happen during surgery and what the nurses would do to prepare me. Before he and Dr. Schroeder left, Dr. Opitz said, "My two little girls are praying for you." As the nurses got me ready, my matted, sand encrusted, dirty hair still clung to my scalp like wallpaper.

I vividly remember my mother's arrival. Like a scene from a movie, the double doors into the ICU separated and she stepped into the room just minutes before they wheeled me out for surgery. Weary and exhausted, she looked small next to the big doors. With only three beds in the room, she immediately found me and started toward my bed. As an independent, 26-year-old, adult woman who traveled around the world by herself, I can honestly say that in my entire life I have never been so happy to see my Mommy. A huge lump surged up in my throat and a barely audible, "Mom" squeaked out. Relief, happiness, anxiety, so many emotions at once, one no stronger than the other. Leaning down over my bedrails, she started crying. Because of the bedrails and my immobility, she could not give me a big hug or scoop me up in her arms and hold me close as I know she wanted to do. She put her hand on my cheek and said to me, "You are the apple of God's eye. He knows you. He knows every hair on your head and has counted them." Giving an ever so slightly nod of recognition and agreement, the nurses came over to take me into surgery. Mom and I squeezed hands, the nurses wheeled me out and Mom remained standing in the ICU.

We think we are so adult and in total control of our own lives. What a myth we all live and attempt to fulfill. The reality is we possess far less control over what happens in our lives. The big, powerful, life-altering experiences that make us feel utterly helpless keep us humble and make us realize we are more childlike than grown up. When hurting and wanting comfort, no matter at what age, the one we long for is a mommy.

The doctors deemed the surgery a success. It lasted about five hours. After opening up my back, the doctors realized, surprisingly, my spinal cord was not severed. As described to me, the cord resembled a rubber band that had stretched out and did not return to its original position. All the nerves inside ripped apart, but the cord itself remained intact. Once they began surgery, they cleared out and flushed away all the bone fragments, and cut some of the muscle away from my vertebrae to fuse T4, T5, T6 and T7 together. To obtain additional bone material for the fusion they removed a piece from my pelvis. For stability, Dr. Opitz placed two Harrington rods about seven inches long on each side of my spine around the break, fused T4 to T7 and held the rods together with screws.

I know all of this in such detail because I actually got to read the surgery report. Before leaving for the States, my doctors gave me all this information and the x-rays. Reading the report fascinated me and satiated my curious nature. It felt a bit odd reading it. The notion that this was not a fictional piece of literature kept creeping into my head. Not only did it really happen, it really happened to me!

The highlight of my post-surgery recovery can be summed up in two words—Morphine Drip. Lying there, relaxed without feeling any pain and being able to move my head and neck more freely. Never before had I taken any narcotic pain relievers. No Codeine. No Vicodin. No Percocet. The occasion never arose, not even when I had my wisdom teeth removed while in college. Being paralyzed helps with feeling no pain; however, the drip played a hefty role too. With all the safety features programmed into the drip, it was impossible to over-medicate myself. No saying silly things, spontaneously bursting into song or having hallucinations. Just being relaxed and primarily using the drip to help me sleep. I remained in ICU after surgery.

With Mom on the scene, Matt and Paula spent less time at the hospital with me. It was time for them to be leaving to re-join the group and continue the trip. I did not want them to go. I have always hated saying goodbye to people, especially when it would be a very long time before seeing them again, if ever. Looking back, I had other reasons for wanting them to stay. They were my friends. Throughout the course of my life, friends have played an integral part, often surrounding me and being involved more than my own family. Sometimes we enjoy the company of friends more than family, or parents for that matter.

I am so thankful and lucky that my mother traveled halfway around the world to be with me. I loved my mother dearly, but had more fun with Matt and Paula. Mom was part of my everyday life. Matt and Paula were part of my fun, traveling life. A link to the life I had known just a few days before, some of the last to know me as a walking person and the first to see me as a person unable to walk. The full magnitude of my not walking did not truly set in because they only saw me lying in a hospital bed, not sitting in a wheelchair cruising around. Knowing something and actually seeing something can be very different experiences. They would walk out of the hospital, I would remain behind, paralyzed. They would resume their lives—traveling, seeing the sights, drinking with the others on the truck—and they would do it without me. At the time I did not recognize this as grief and the start of mourning an unfathomable loss.

Matt and Paula left on the morning of Monday, April 20, a week and a day after my accident. They came to my room early before Mom got to the hospital. Paula reached into her bag and pulled out a box. An unexpected parting gift. I eagerly flipped open the lid and the face of a Mickey

Mouse wrist watch on a shiny black watchband stared at me. While at the hospital, unable to turn my head to see a clock, I constantly asked Matt and Paula for the time. Paula helped me put it on. The watch looked a bit juvenile with bright silver-colored Mickey Mouse ears jutting off from the top of the face, but I loved it. I wore it for the rest of my hospital stay.

It was not a Timex, but that baby took a lickin' and kept on tickin'. The battery and wrist band were replaced so many times that I lost track. It possessed such significance and sentimental value that I wore it for the next six years and got loads of compliments on it. Unfortunately the day finally arrived when the watch met its demise. At tennis practice while bringing my racquet down to hit the ball, I hit my wrist and smashed the face of it beyond repair. Staring down at the smashed face, a wave of disappointment washed over me. Pushing over to the courtside trash can, I tossed it in without much hesitation. The time had come to let it go.

After they gave me the watch, we said our goodbyes. There was not much else to say at this point. They each gave me a kiss, turned and started to walk out of the room. A few steps away from my bed, Matt turned back, gave me one more kiss on the lips and they walked out the door. Then I cried for the first time. Not a deep, let-it-all-out, soulful grieving kind of cry (that would come later, much later) as if I had been holding it all in until that point. But rather shedding tears of sadness for my friends leaving. We would simply not see each other again in a few weeks or even months. My life would be significantly different and forever changed by the accident on the sand dune. They would leave, rejoin the group and carry on with their travels. I remained behind to embark on a journey I had never wanted to start.

During recovery, Dr. Schroeder visited the hospital every day, twice a day. He said it surprised him that my spinal cord was not severed. Being colonized by the Dutch, Namibia is a very Christian country. Even the way they practice medicine differs from the States. Dr. Schroeder openly and comfortably said, "There are some cases, where I did two percent of the work and God did the other ninety eight percent". In terms of the body healing, Dr. Schroeder said to allow my body seven years to heal itself. Not that I would be totally healed in seven years, but some things may change and the possibility existed to regain some function. It was still too early to tell.

This philosophy sits in stark contrast to anything here in the States. "Whatever you do not get back in a year, won't come back at all," is what doctors tell patients here. I have learned that not to be true. Granted, doctors do not want to give people false hope. Have I regained any function? No, not in the sensation and movement sense; however, my body started giving me more signals a few years after my accident. Paralysis forces me to pay attention to what my body may be saying. For instance, now my body tells me (most of the time) when I have to pee. Until about seven years post-injury, I rarely had any signals. Once in a while, my face would get a little hot or my nose would turn red, but that was about it. Now, when I feel certain muscle spasms and tingling sensations, that is my cue.

With my spine now stabilized, Dr. Schroeder fitted me

with a back brace to wear only during the recovery period, not permanently. The brace went around my chest and had a chin and head support so the weight of my head did not press upon my healing vertebrae when sitting up. His particular brace turned out to be better than anything I would have gotten in the States. Usually all patients are given a tortoise shell brace—two pieces of thick plastic that Velcro together to encapsulate the body. That brace starts at one's hips and rises up to the sternum. My brace was smaller, with full coverage in back, but crisscrossed in front. What a godsend for women because the tortoise shell style uncomfortably mashed down their boobs.

After Matt and Paula left, only Mom kept me company. She arrived in the morning and spent all day with me, never wanting to leave. She read me stories from the Bible. Before and during the divorce, Mom had been part of the Bible Study Fellowship International program which revitalized her faith. Even though we were a family of faith, we never talked much about the power of Jesus or quoted the Bible in our house. Catholics are generally not known for their Bible quoting ability. While living with Mom before my African adventure, she quoted more Bible verses in one year than I had heard from her my entire life. Not sharing the same religious fervor as her, I'd simply roll my eyes. Here it was different. She started sharing her resurrected faith and it comforted me. No eye rolling this time. Here we were, a mother reading to her child, sharing her faith. How many years had it been since she read stories to me, let alone, stories from the Bible? Probably 20. I liked it. These words and unshakable faith demonstrated by Mom gave me far more strength than I acknowledged at the time.

I remained in ICU for a few days after surgery. With rods in my back and my spine stabilized, Judy, the ICU nurse, approached my bed and cheerfully announced, "We finally get to wash your hair!" Oh, what joy! Remembering trips to the hair salon for a cut, the best part was the hair wash and scalp massage. It felt marvelously relaxing and always seemed to end too soon. After having matted, dirty, gross hair for over a week, feeling the warm water saturate my scalp and the nurse vigorously scrub behind my neck and ears was the closest I would come to ecstasy any time soon. Talk about having an appreciation for the small things in life. After three washes, my hair and scalp were finally squeaky clean.

To prevent pressure sores from developing, the nurses started turning me and propping me up on my side. This could not be done before surgery because of my broken spine. Without moving around and taking pressure off areas of skin, the skin can start to break down due to lack of blood and oxygen flow to that area. When a body possesses full feeling, it provides signals when it needs to move, like when a leg gets stiff or when an arm falls asleep. Areas with little muscle, fat or other tissue between the skin and bone can be particularly problematic, like the hip bone when lying on one's side. As a paralyzed person, I do not feel such signals and do not know if blood flow to certain areas diminishes, so I have to physically move myself or have someone do it for me as was the case while recovering from surgery.

Early on the second Saturday after my surgery, the nurses

propped me up to lie on my left side. I faced the empty bed next to me and read a book. Suddenly, paramedics crashed through the ICU doors pushing a man on a gurney. The nurses quickly whipped the separation curtain shut. Although it was mostly closed, I could still peer in an opening to see the gruesome scene. It felt like being on the set of *ER*. Nurses and paramedics surrounded this body with a bloody and lacerated face.

The man lived. With everything finished and under control, I noticed that one of the paramedics was Craig, the Richie Cunningham look-a-like who had rescued me from the bottom of the sand dune. He came 'round to my side of the curtain to say hello. He did not know it, but he had a fine splattering of blood on his face, as if someone had misted him with a squirt bottle of red paint. I asked what happened, and Craig said the guy was driving down the road and either hit a kudu or the kudu had run up on top of the hood of his car and crushed the top of the car down on the guy. A kudu is a wild animal and about the size of a big stag or a small moose. In lay terms, it's a big-assed animal. The accident had left the man in a coma. The paramedics brought him to the Medi Clinic hospital because it was closest. Since he did not have private insurance, once his system stabilized, he was moved to a government-run hospital. I do not know what happened after the move.

To pass the time after surgery I decided to send a letter to loads of people to tell them what happened. Unable to write from a horizontal position, I dictated and Mom wrote. At that time, I kept in touch with many people from my travels and friends back home. The words describing the accident easily rolled off my tongue; remembering nearly every detail quite clearly without getting emotional or upset, very much like being at the bottom of the dune. While not difficult for me, I wonder if it was hard for Mom to write it. During the time we spent together in the hospital, Mom never asked about my trip. This has always puzzled me. Having completed two months of my amazing African adventure, I had some stories to tell, but Mom never asked anything about it. Maybe she thought talking about it would upset me or she thought it might upset her. I never regretted taking the trip, not even for a nanosecond. I wanted to tell her about all the great people I met and what we did, but she appeared to have no interest. So I never talked about any of it.

Before leaving the States for this trip, I had a rough sketch of what would happen when the Drago adventure ended—flying from Cape Town, South Africa up to Ireland for three months to stay with Mary, a friend from high school who lived on the west side of the country near Galway. I had planned to fly up to London, book a flight to Ireland, then phone up Mary to let her know when I would arrive. After discovering what happened, she called me in Namibia from Ireland. Asking her how she found out, she said, "My mom called and left a message saying, 'call me when you get this, it's about Jocelyn.'" Immediately Mary thought "Great, she's not coming. I line up a job and a place for her to live and she's not coming." Well, she was correct in that, but completely shocked when she heard why.

Penny also received the letter. She was my friend from

Western Australia whom I lived with for two months while working at her family's plant nursery. In the months following my accident, I spoke with her on the phone. She told me she had received my letter early in the day but wanted time to read it slowly and enjoy it. She said, "You always wrote such good letters, I did not want to rush through it." She waited until crawling into bed for some evening reading. Anticipating a description of my latest adventure or a boy story, she could not believe the words staring at her on the page. She got out of bed, wandered down and stood silently in the doorway of her parents' bedroom. By the look on her face they knew something terrible had happened.

About a week after surgery I moved out of ICU because the hospital needed the bed for someone in a more serious condition. Being in a new unit meant a new group of nurses to care for me. Some nurses and nurse aides came from the native Namibian tribes. When speaking to each other, they spoke in their own tribal languages. When speaking to non-natives they spoke English and Afrikaans, a variation from the Dutch language. The first time two nurses entered my room they started speaking Afrikaans to me. Seeing a fair-skinned woman with blonde hair and blue eyes, they assumed I was a local and spoke the language. I smiled and almost on the verge of laughter said, "English, please. I'm American." They responded by giggling then started speaking English. When the nurses bathed me and changed my bedding they conversed in their tribal language. Not understanding anything, I listened, engrossed in the unique and interesting sounds of their language. One sound that fascinated me most was this clicking/popping noise which came from the back of the throat. It sounded like the noise from the lollipop song made by putting your finger in your mouth and snapping it out against your cheek.

By the time I entered the new ward, the other American girl had gone back to the States. Whew! No chance of sharing a room with her again. My dedicated mother literally spent the entire day at my side from morning 'til night. Bierta, the physiotherapist, would come and stretch my legs every day so that my muscles would not become stiff. She also left some arm weights with me to start arm exercises. Every now and then, Mom would pick up my leg and she said they were already smaller—from atrophy I suppose. At that point, two weeks after my accident, I had not yet sat up in a wheelchair. Even in bed, Dr. Schroeder wanted me up at only a 45 degree angle to keep pressure off my healing spine.

Rather than being cooped up inside the entire day, Mom wanted me to get outside in the sunshine. Being on the edge of a desert, Windhoek saw a great deal of sunshine. Going outside in a wheelchair was not an option. But, my determined mother found a way! The hospital bed in which I lay just happened to be on wheels. She asked if my entire bed, with me in it, could be wheeled outside. The staff agreed it could indeed. One of the orderlies released the brakes on my hospital bed, slowly wheeled me down the hall and took me outside to a secluded concrete courtyard area. The sun nearly blinded me as the doors parted and the rays bounced off the pale cement. At that point I had not been outside for two weeks—highly uncharacteristic. Feeling the first penetrating rays of the glorious sunshine gave me goose bumps. Once those faded, the warmth felt glorious on my skin. My nostrils filled with the hot smell of sun-baked, gritty concrete. How marvelous to be outside again!

Aside from my daily visits by Dr. Schroeder and Mom, I did have other visitors—a few people from the American Embassy and two officers from the U.S. Army, Captain Darrell Singer, MD and Chief Warrant Officer 2 Donald Bellinger. Although I did not have much interaction with the Embassy, they had very much helped Matt and my mother. One woman from the Embassy wanted to take my mom out shopping just for a change of scenery and something else to do. Mom did not want to leave my side—bless her, but I wanted her to, even if for only a little while.

Yes, even with a broken back and paralysis, I learned that some things about me did not and would not change. While a very social person, I also need alone time and was desperately craving it. I wanted my mother to leave, go shopping, go for a walk or do something other than sit next to me. I love her dearly and so appreciated her dedication, but desired some time to myself. Never had I spent so much time with one person, not only 12+ hours each day, but for two weeks each and every day. It was driving me nuts. As a child and being home with Mom, we would be under the same roof, but not right next to each other all day. Even on the Drago truck, I spent long periods of time driving with the same people, but I would move around and talk to different people throughout the day. Even Matt and Paula left for brief periods in the day. Not that I wanted her to leave so that I could break down and let out some emotion. We simply needed a break from each other.

Eventually, Mom had to go shopping to buy some clothes for me to travel back to the States. Since they had cut my clothes off in the emergency room, I'd worn not a stitch of clothing for my entire hospital stay. Sheets and blankets covered me, but no hospital gown. To bathe me and not have to move me around too much because of my new spinal fusion, it was easier to have me wear nothing. They did not have to worry about my getting up and walking around the hospital naked.

With my fusion healing and strength increasing, my time drew near to leave Windhoek. The way it worked out with her ticket, Mom, very apprehensively, left a few days before me. It did not bother me a bit. A few days by myself sounded heavenly.

*"Times have changed, times are strange
Here I come, but I ain't the same,
Mama, I'm coming home."*

—*Mama, I'm Coming Home* by Ozzy Ozbourne

Chapter Four
Homeward Bound

Well on my way down Recovery Road and with my spine stabilized, it came time to return to the States. There I would start rehabilitation and learn how to live with my new limitations. Bierta, my physical therapist, stretched my legs everyday and gave me hand weights and exercises to do while lying down in bed. Women do not have the natural arm and shoulder strength men have, so we have to work harder to build up muscle. Developing my arm strength just scratched the surface of all the new things I would have to learn to do.

With Mom now gone, I occupied myself with arm exercises, reading and listening to the tapes I had with me on my Walkman. Boy, doesn't that date me? Before the days of iPods, MP3 players and even portable CD players, there was the Walkman. A handheld portable device with headphones powered by AA batteries which played cassette tapes. The younger generation of today cannot even conceive of a Walkman, let alone cassette tapes.

Knowing I would want lots of musical variety on my trip, but unwilling to carry loads of tapes, I had made three mixed tapes for my journey. One guy on the truck, Axel from the Netherlands, borrowed my favorite mix when the truck stopped in Windhoek. People gave me compliments on my mixes; I felt flattered he wanted to borrow it. That afternoon Paula and I saw Axel as we walked back from the grocery store to the hostel where we stayed. He said his knapsack had been stolen off his bed through a window. Someone had reached through with a long object and made off with his bag. What a bummer! His camera and Walkman had been in the bag. After he mentioned his Walkman, I impulsively blurted out, "Oh, no, my tape was in it!" *Dammit*, I thought, *that tape was my favorite*. He felt bad because my tape was gone. I felt bad because he certainly suffered the greater loss. He appreciated my empathy. So, during my hospital stay, I alternated between my two remaining tapes.

Thanks to my outstanding support network—Matt and Paula, Mom, my sister, Dad and friends back home—all the arrangements with the insurance companies, hospitals, rehab center and flying home were sorted without my lifting a finger. Thankfully I did not have to deal with being newly paralyzed and all the other subsequent matters as did my American roommate-for-a-day. All the initial phone calls Matt had made to the travel insurance companies facilitated my travel plans back to the States. Once Dr. Schroeder gave the approval to fly home, the evacuation insurance company worked out the travel arrangements with my family. Shortly before leaving Windhoek, I learned that once in Kalamazoo, I would be taken to Mary Free Bed Rehabilitation Hospital in Grand Rapids, Michigan, nationally recognized for its work in spinal cord injury rehabilitation. While Gretchen took on other responsibilities, Dad investigated Mary Free Bed and made the arrangements for my admission. How lucky to have such a nationally renowned rehab center only one hour north of Kalamazoo.

Upon learning where I would do my spinal rehab once back in the States, I did not worry, fret and wonder about the many unknowns ahead of me. What would rehab be like and what would I learn? How drastically different would life be? To maintain sanity and not pre-determine my fate by imagining answers to so many questions, I focused on the next, more tangible, immediate thing. Would Bierta give me more exercises to do? Would I try sitting up on the edge of the bed today with my back brace on? Would I get to go outside in the courtyard? Exactly how would I fly home and with whom? At the moment, the next big thing was Mom's journey back home. When Mom left, only a few days before me, I did not yet know any details about my flight back, other than that a nurse and a paramedic from London were flying down to Windhoek to accompany me home on the plane.

Another question people often ask me is, "Did you have insurance? Who covered your medical bills? Was any part of your accident covered by insurance?" The short answer is yes. To go on this particular overland trip, Dragoman required that each person take out medical travel insurance and evacuation insurance policies. I had purchased similar medical policies for my trips to Europe and New Zealand. The evacuation insurance enabled a policy holder to be flown home from anywhere in the world and covered up to $25,000. I took out the highest possible policy coverage, which cost a few hundred dollars, for the medical travel insurance which would cover up to $11,000 in expenses. The evacuation insurance covered the majority of the costs to get me home, but Mom had to put another $3,000 on her credit card to cover the costs. The insurance company charged her card the $3,000, but when the bill came it reflected the charge and, strangely, a credit for $3,000. It was very odd, but God does work in very mysterious ways. I remember signing the policy papers and thinking, *What a pain in the ass this is, I am never going to need these policies.* Ha, what did I know?

In hindsight, one of the smartest decisions I ever made was to sell my car before my trip to keep a health insurance policy active. Prior to leaving for Africa, I had health insurance through a COBRA policy from my dad's employer. At the time the premium cost just over a $150 each month (this was the late 90's after all). Since I would be away for six months—three in Africa, three in Ireland—it meant I would pay about $1,000 to keep up my COBRA payments and retain my policy while away. My trip to Africa had cost me enough already and I had spent most of my cash on the trip. The only thing I possessed of any real value was my car. I loved my car. A chic cream colored, 4-door, 1985 Chevy Celebrity that had been a hand-me-down from my Grandpa Dettloff. It had its quirks, like the heat being on year round, but it heated up nearly instantly in the coldest of temps. It did not have air conditioning so I drove on the highway with the back windows down for ventilation because keeping the front windows open produced way too much wind. Very basic, no power windows or locks. Sometimes it would not start and I had to get under the hood and stick a screwdriver in this one spot to hold open a flap which acted as a manual choke for the car. It worked like a charm every time.

I vividly remember the winter of 1993/94. It sticks in my mind so well because it was the winter before I left for New Zealand. I worked at Real Seafood and lived far off campus. We experienced some frigid, bone chilling air that year. Driving home late one night after work, the light from the street lights was coming straight down—like "beam me up Scotty" from Star Trek. The temperature sank to a cool -55 degrees F with the wind chill factor. I had never seen anything like it before. As someone later explained to me, the air was so cold that the light particles could not disperse. Loads of people became stranded because they could not start their cars. AAA Michigan had a day and a half waiting list for a jump start. After those record cold temps subsided, AAA took out a full page ad in the *Detroit Free Press* apologizing to their clients/members. But, my little baby started up every morning like a champ—and I even parked outside!

So in thinking about my beloved automobile, I could:

1) Drop the insurance and keep the car for when I got back from Ireland—I was young, healthy and hardly ever went to the doctor.

2) Sell my car to keep up the COBRA payments— six months was a long time and who could say what would happen in six months. I could decide to stay in Ireland.

Luckily, I chose to sell my car and keep my health insurance. I sold the car myself. Never having done this before, I did not even know how much to ask for it. It was January and my departure date was in February, so I wanted to get rid of it fast. Aside from its quirks, it was a good car. I listed it for $1,000 and probably could have listed it for more; live and learn. The day after putting the ad in the paper, I received about ten calls. Victor phoned first and thus test drove it first. He had just moved up from Mexico to join his family. After taking it for a spin, he offered me $750 and I countered with $850. Sold!

We all get very attached to our cars, but I felt especially connected to mine. A year after my accident I finally purchased a car, thanks to a fundraiser my high school had for me. A 1998 Pontiac Grand Prix. Never in my life had I been able to write a check for a car and I probably never will again. Even though I lived in Grand Rapids then, I purchased the car in Kalamazoo, and had the hand controls installed in Kalamazoo too. Mom drove the car from the dealership to the adaptation garage, one of the few times I rode as a passenger in my car. Gretchen followed us in her car so we would not have to wait at the garage.

The next few hours crept along at a snail's pace. The anticipation of driving and having my own vehicle was like being 16 all over again. Finally we returned to the garage. I quickly got in and sat there marveling at my car, caressing and gripping my steering wheel, running my hand over the gear shift and testing out the hand controls while my car remained stationary. Like a gear shift jutting out from the left side of the steering wheel, I pulled the hand control lever toward the floor for the gas and pushed it toward the dashboard for the brake. Everything appeared to be in working order. Easing out of the parking space, I slowly approached the driveway, excited and a bit nervous all at the same time.

Watching cars pass, I waited for traffic to clear to make

a left turn onto the road. A cream colored Celebrity came toward me from the right. It looked very much like the one I once owned. Then I saw the University of Michigan sticker in its back window. My eyes darted to find the driver. There sat Victor! Unbelievable! The garage and Mom's house, where Victor purchased the car, were nowhere near each other in Kalamazoo. I sat there stunned and could not believe that on the very day I picked up my new car to begin my attachment with it, I see my old car one last time. My heart ached for a moment remembering what a great car she was. Snapping back to the present, taking in the look and the smell of my new baby, when the traffic finally cleared, I sped out onto the road. Yep, I'd love this one too.

** ** ** ** ** **

Two days before my departure from the hospital in Windhoek I had a hospital room to myself. Four beds were in the room, just no roommates for me. I had been reading when the phone rang at about 8:00 P.M. Mom had left by this time so it surprised me.

"Hello," I said tentatively.

"Jocelyn, it is Dr. Schroder. Are you watching television?"

"No, not right now."

"Please, turn on the TV, there is something interesting I want you to see." Without giving me any details, he hung up.

I placed the handset back in the cradle, grabbed the remote, and turned on the TV. Cable and satellite dishes had not yet hit Windhoek; only four channels were available on the hospital TV system. A basketball game was in progress, but not just any basketball game—a wheelchair basketball game. I watched it for a big whopping ten seconds (if even that long), said "fuck that" and with a big sigh turned off the TV. De Nile ain't just a river in Egypt. I did not spend much time in the early days thinking about what my life might be like long range or what I ultimately would and would not be able to do. If they wanted to play basketball, yippie skip for them. I did not care much for basketball before I broke my back and certainly could not see myself suddenly wanting to play the sport using a wheelchair. Even though I felt motivated to begin physical therapy and was coping well, looking back, I see this as a starting point for the depression which would ensue. More on this later.

During his visit the next morning, Dr. Schroder mentioned the basketball game. He had to bring it up, because I did not. Since I watched it only for a few seconds, I was not sure what to say. He said, "I wanted to show you what is possible even though you are not able to walk. You can lead a normal life." Unprompted by me, he went on to say, "Good sex always happens from what is between your ears, not between your legs." Until that point I had not even thought about how sex would be different, or dating, or having children. I was not dating anyone at the time of my accident, in a steady relationship or "getting any" on a regular basis. I suppose that is why sex was not on the forefront of my concerns. I was focused on other, more immediate things, like sitting up for the first time, putting my back brace on, flying home, and starting rehab in Grand Rapids.

The day before my departure, two nurses were in my room turning me in bed. Suddenly a man and woman walked in as if they had reached their targeted destination. I thought it a bit strange since I had no idea who they were. Once the nurses got me settled, they introduced themselves; Ruth, the nurse, and Peter, the paramedic, who would escort me home on the plane. Both were British and had flown down from London. Ruth, in her late 30's, with short auburn/ brown hair, was friendly, chatty and warm which made me feel very comfortable. Peter, in his 40's and the quieter of the two, possessed a serenity I found calming. One of Ruth's first questions was, "Are you on any medication at all?" Since the morphine drip, the doctor had given me no other pain killers or medication. When I replied, "No," she smiled and said definitively, "Good, then you can have a drink on the plane, luv." God I love those Brits! After drinking practically every night on the truck, then having nothing for weeks, a drink sounded good.

They did not stay in the room with me long. Right from the Windhoek airport they'd popped over to the hospital to meet me and suss out the situation. The next day or two would be long days for them, so after a quick greeting, they headed to their lodgings. As I would discover later in the many hours I spent with them, Peter and Ruth traveled together often on trips like this. They traveled to destinations all over the world and flew home with injured or seriously hurt people who needed medical supervision. Even from my brief contact with them at this point, I could tell they made a great team, like two cops who have been partners for years. They were friendly, relaxed and very respectful of one another. Even though I just met them, I felt comfortable and confident to be in their hands.

The next day, May 4, the flight took off in the evening. I spent the day preparing for the journey. Before Mom flew home, she left me at the hospital during the day only once, to buy clothes for me to wear home. Though Matt had grabbed my rucksack from the truck and given it to my mother, all my clothes were so grubby from the trip, Mom wanted to get me something new (and clean) to wear home. She purchased a navy blue sweat suit for me with a hooded zip front sweat shirt. When the nurses finally had me dressed, one of the ICU nurses came in to say goodbye. She did a double take and said, "Oh, I hardly even recognized you with proper clothes on." Everyone had grown accustomed to seeing me with only a sheet covering me. Plus, I lost a bit of weight, my hair grew and the bruising from my black eye faded. I looked quite different from the girl who arrived with a broken back just a few weeks ago.

Dr. Schroder came in to say good-bye—and to hand me his bill. Everyone had a separate bill for me; Dr. Schroder for his medical supervision and visits, Dr. Opitz for the surgery, and Bierta for her physiotherapy. How much was Dr. Schroder's bill? Keep in mind that I stayed in the hospital for three weeks, and Dr. Schroder came to see me twice a day and assisted with the surgery. He handed me the bill. I unfolded it and looked at it in stunned silence. He said, "No doctor in the States would work for this." His bill totaled $10,000 ND (Namib dollars). While that may sound like a significant amount of money, the exchange rate at the time was 1 USD = 4 ND, so the bill for three weeks of his services came to about $2,500. Hence the reason for my stunned silence. The bill for the Medi Clinic itself for ICU, my bed in another ward, meals, etc…came to $55,000 ND or roughly $12,000 USD. One day in a U.S. hospital could exceed that amount.

Until now, Peter and Ruth had told me nothing of the preparation process for the flight. Getting me ready was not as simple as throwing some clothes on me and transferring me onto a gurney. Even though the surgery stabilized my spine and I had to wear a brace when fully sitting up, I would be flat on my back on a stretcher for the trip home, the entire trip, not just to get from the hospital to the airport, but all the way back to the States. Ruth and Peter wanted to make sure that no additional jarring or movement would take place when transporting me. Yes, I had rods and metal in my back, but with a new fusion, they did not want anything else to happen.

Before moving me from the bed, Ruth and Peter explained the process. They put me on a stretcher inside what looked to be a deflated rubber raft. As they laid me in the bottom of the raft, I squeezed the side of it. It felt like the little Styrofoam pellets inside a bean bag, kind of squishy, yet with a certain density to it. Then they turned on a little machine and instead of blowing air into the raft to inflate it, the machine sucked out the air to vacuum pack me in. I was as snug as a bug in a rug. Me or my spine would not be moving one iota. It was not uncomfortable exactly, I just could not move much.

Hell, other than my arms, I had not been able to move much the past few weeks anyway. While I was well packed for the trip from the hospital to the airport, Ruth reassured me she would loosen things up on the plane so I would not be that snug for the entire journey home.

As they packed me in and started wheeling me out of the hospital room, the phone rang one final time. One of the nurses answered it and I asked who it was. The nurse said, "It's Judy from Ann Arbor." I had worked with her at Real Seafood until I left for New Zealand and Oz in 1994. I stretched out my hand as best I could so the nurse could pass me the phone. This was the first time that Judy had called, so I at least wanted to say hello. I put the phone to my ear and said, "Schmude!!" (her nickname) and explained why I could not talk at the moment. Since phone calls had flooded in my first day in the hospital, rather fitting I would exit with one. The nurses and I said our final good-byes, and we left.

Gliding down the hall, packed in tight on the gurney, I bid farewell to a place I would never return—the moment when paralysis began. Never again would I hold a place in this world as a walking person. Many challenges awaited me back home, so many inconceivable to me at the time. But keeping focused on the next thing helped me to move on and look to the future instead of staring back at the past.

The next task involved getting to the airport. Peter and Ruth rode with me in the back of an ambulance which resembled more of an oversized station wagon as it was a bit shallow and cramped in the back. By this time the day had grown dark. The ambulance pulled up to the curb and Peter hopped out to get the luggage checked and tickets organized. In all my travels, I had never seen anyone being flown on a stretcher on a commercial aircraft, and I had no idea how it would be done. While Peter was inside, Ruth explained to me that the last six rows on one side of the plane would be blocked off for me and the stretcher would be set on top of the seat backs. She was a pro at this, so she knew what she was talking about.

After about 20 minutes, Peter returned and crawled into the ambulance. Ruth asked, "Did everything get sorted?"

"Yes," he said with a peculiar tone in his voice. "This bloke, the ticket agent, got Joce all set with the stretcher and the rows of seats. Then he went to get our seats arranged and asked, 'And where would you like to sit?' The look I must have given him. I said, 'With her, where else?'" The ticket agent probably thought Peter and Ruth would dump me in back, sit somewhere else and get pissed on the flight home. The Windhoek airport most likely did not get many passengers flying on stretchers. I knew Peter and Ruth would be with me throughout my trip. It never entered my mind, nor theirs, that we would be separated from each other.

The flight route home was Windhoek to Frankfurt, Germany, with a one-hour layover in Frankfurt, then on to London with a five-hour layover at Heathrow, then to Detroit, Michigan. An ambulance would be waiting for me at Detroit Metro Airport to take me to Willow Run airport in Ypsilanti for the short flight to Kalamazoo. It sounded like an awfully long journey. Once we were airborne and settled in, Ruth asked, "So, luv, what would you like to drink?"

Even though I developed a fancy for Gin and Tonics while in Africa, a Bloody Mary sounded the best. So, that is what she got me and yes, there really was alcohol in it.

That flight home was probably one of the only times I slept semi-comfortably on a plane. For once I could stretch out. Everything went smoothly. When we arrived at Heathrow we had five hours to kill. Heathrow received passengers on stretchers often and knew exactly what to do. They even had a medical center at the airport. From the plane I went in an ambulance to the med center. Ruth and Peter moved me out of the rubber raft, onto a bed and propped me up on my side for a while to get me off my back to prevent pressure marks on my skin. When we left Heathrow for Detroit, Ruth and Peter did not know if their journey with me would end in Detroit or if they would travel with me all the way to Kzoo. Landing at Detroit Metro Airport with a stretcher passenger was a new experience for both of them. They wanted to have confidence in the competence of those taking over stateside.

At Heathrow we boarded a brand new (just three weeks old) British Airways Boeing 777. Wow, it even smelled new like that fresh new-car smell. The fabric preserver, hot-off-the-assembly-line chemicals still lingered in the air. This new plane even had a wheelchair accessible bathroom. Not that I had the opportunity to use it, but the crew made sure to point it out to me. I slept for most of the flight. As we approached Detroit, the pilot gave his landing preparation and final message to the passengers. He wished people well on their further travels and added, "Especially those lying down." That brought a big smile to my face.

While the staff at Heathrow expertly and efficiently handled loading and unloading stretchers off planes, the staff at Detroit Metro did not. I do not think any of them ever had a stretcher come in on a plane, let alone have to get one off. Thankfully, Ruth and Peter remained at my side. After all the other passengers disembarked, airport personnel, firemen and an American paramedic came on board, but no one knew what to do or how to get me off the plane whilst still on the stretcher. No one consulted Peter, Ruth or me. They talked to each other at the front of the plane, talked to their cohorts on radios, walked up the aisle past me to the back of the plane and talked some more to each other and on their radios. Imagine Tweedledum and Tweedledee trying to solve a crisis. This chaos did not make a stellar impression on Peter and Ruth.

Not wanting to come off as the foreigners who knew it all (bless those Brits), Ruth and Peter sat back and did not say anything right away. Within minutes, an Air Med team from the University of Michigan arrived to take me to Willow Run airport in Ypsilanti. They took charge of things. After the Air Med team arrived, Ruth and Peter felt more confident about my care the rest of the way home. The three of us knew then that Ruth and Peter's journey with me would end in Detroit. I parted ways with my guardians as they delivered me to the next set to finish my journey home. I have never seen or heard from them again. It's just the nature of their job.

As the plane touched down in Kzoo, I felt little joy or relief. The closer I drew to my old stomping ground, the heavier the weight of my new reality became. I was coming home to my

95

roots, but I was not the same, nor would I ever be. Sure, I'd come back from my other trips changed in ways; a change in my perspective, a little heavier from the good beer, or speaking with a new rhythm and new words in my vocabulary. But nothing like this. I would never look the same or do things in the same way. While the other experiences from my travels changed me on the inside, this adventure transformed me on the outside for the entire world to see. Crossing over the threshold of my accident, a door had slammed shut behind me. With no window in the door and the heaviness swelling on my shoulders and in my heart, I could not look back, but only move forward.

Other than the givens—Mom, Gretch and my brother-in-law, Tim, I did not know who would be awaiting my arrival at the Kzoo airport or the hospital. However, I did know for certain who would not be there—Dad. In a way, it did reduce some stress in an already anxious situation. Gretchen and I would not have to deal with the tension of having our parents together. They finalized their divorce in January, 1997. Mom did not want to be around Dad. Even though Gretch and I had been speaking to Dad through this ordeal, our individual relationships with him were far from reconciled. When he had called me in Windhoek, we stuck to the facts at hand.

Before leaving Windhoek, he informed me he would have to work the evening of my return. As an Urban Planner, he often attended evening meetings. That particular evening he needed to give some presentation or pitch a proposal to a potential client. I realize the importance of jobs and bringing home a pay check. Growing up my sister and I often heard,

"I'm sorry, I have to work" when Dad missed some activity in which Gretch or I participated. However, given the magnitude of the situation, his younger daughter paralyzed from an accident that happened on the other side of the world, I hoped he would be there. I wished he would cancel his presentation. Get someone to fill in for him or reschedule it. Just like the feeling of relief at seeing my mommy come through the ICU doors in Windhoek, I felt like a little girl who simply wanted her daddy to come and make everything all better. I wanted him to do something to show his daughter would be his number one priority. But he did not. While my body has physically healed and much spiritual, internal healing has occurred, I have never fully recovered from this wound. I truly believe the fear and anxiety he felt about seeing all of us, and other family friends at the hospital who were furious with my dad for this divorce, engulfed him. He could not be there for my sake; he was too focused on how it would impact him.

Mom and Gretch greeted me at the airport. Everyone else waited at the hospital. As I discovered later, my sister felt very apprehensive about seeing me because she did not know how I would look. Yes, she spoke with me on the phone, but speaking to me knowing I'm paralyzed and actually seeing me paralyzed are two very different things. They took the gurney off the plane. Because of my fusion and not wearing my brace, I could not raise or move my head very much. Gretch smiled, leaned over me as much as she could due to the gurney railing between us, and we gave each other air kisses on each cheek, our impression of hoity toity women greeting each other when they do not want to smudge their lipstick. We used to do it as a joke when saying hello or goodbye.

From the airport an ambulance transported me to the Trauma Center at Bronson Hospital in downtown Kalamazoo. Gretchen's husband, Tim, waited at the hospital, along with Al and Rita who were longtime family friends; Al had been Gretchen's and my pediatrician. Rita had come over to Mom's house on April 14 to support her and assist in making the arrangements to travel to Namibia.

Lying down so much really skewed my perspective. I vividly remember being wheeled into the hospital, Rita looking down at me with tears in her eyes and gently touching my face as if I were her own daughter. She had known me since I was seven years old. Tim's best friend, Rich, who lived in Chicago, was also there. He had driven in after work that night to see me. Back in February, my flight for Africa had left from Chicago's O'Hare Airport. I stayed at Rich's place the night before I left, and he took me to the airport the next day. He waited with me until my plane boarded. The agent took my boarding pass, checked me in. I turned one last time to wave at Rich, then walked through the door and down the jet way, the last time he saw me walking. These people came to show their support, but my father did not.

I arrived at the hospital sometime in the evening. The sun was no longer visible, but the last rays of the day lit the sky. They settled me into a room with two beds, but no roommate. Everyone stayed only a little while. They knew I was wiped out from the 36-hour trip back to the States. Without exerting myself and lying down the entire time I do not know how I could have been tired, but I was. After everyone else said their goodbyes, my sister lingered, and I sensed she did not want to leave. She grew silent. I looked at her and she started crying. Between the two of us, she is more sensitive and more easily shows her emotion. Even though I traveled across the world to go to Africa by myself and relished my few quiet days on my own after my mother left Windhoek, Gretchen did not want to leave me, her little sister, alone. I reassured her that I would be fine and she should not worry about me. My consolation made her feel better. She dried her tears and kissed me goodbye. I was home.

Medically, the doctor at Bronson could not do much for me. He primarily monitored me to make sure my vitals remained stable. Mom and other family members expressed optimism that returning to the States would allow me access to some procedure or knowledge that could instigate some healing of my spinal cord. This was not the case. The treatments for spinal cord injuries are the same in Namibia as in the States. Typically, steroids are administered immediately to reduce swelling in the spinal cord. But nerves within my spinal cord ripped apart. No treatment existed anywhere in the world to repair damaged spinal cord nerves. Not once did I think *if only the accident had happened in the U.S., I would not be paralyzed,* or *if the accident happened in a more urban setting with quicker medical rescue/response, I would not be paralyzed.* Bronson was simply another layover stop on my way to Mary Free Bed in Grand Rapids.

My first full day at Bronson resembled my first day at the

hospital in Windhoek. This time, instead of having loads of callers on the phone, my day bustled with visitors. Jackie and Lori, who had worked with me in the office where I had been a receptionist before my African trip, came by to see me. Jackie and I got along really well. Had we met at different times in our lives, we probably would have become really good friends. When we met, she was married and pregnant with their first child, and I would not be staying in Kalamazoo. Jackie knew I was a Rod Stewart fan, so she brought me one of those stand-up cardboard figures of Rod and put it in my hospital room. With all the visitors who stopped by, I saw apprehension and awkwardness on their faces. However, after seeing and speaking to me for a few minutes, it all melted away.

Rich stopped by on his way back to Chicago. Jeff, a fellow bartender from Applebee's, also stopped to see me. Gretch was there most of the day. There was a brief time when Rich, Jeff and Gretch were all there at the same time. After the guys left, she commented, "Could you feel the testosterone in the room?" I was a little puzzled by her comment and did not understand what she meant. Essentially she meant that when the guys were in the room together there was an understated "pissing contest" between the two vying for my attention or who could do the most for me. If Jeff sat closer to me than Rich, Rich would ask if he could get me anything. If one moved away from me the other moved closer. Rich had to get going back to Chicago, but neither of the guys wanted to be the first one to leave. Tending to be rather oblivious to such things, if Gretchen had not pointed it out, I would never have noticed. My sister always really liked Jeff and thought we should date. I liked Jeff too, but not in the dating kind of way.

Finally, my dad came by to see me after the lunch hour visitor rush. He brought bright, yellow flowers with him. Whether a card, flowers, balloons or cardboard cut-out of my favorite musicians, just about everyone brought something for me. It felt like everyone wanted to do something for me or at least put a smile on my face. However, there was nothing, medically, anyone could do for me, so they did for me what was within their power to do.

With a light tap on the open hospital room door announcing his arrival, Dad entered slowly carrying the yellow flowers. Once he was in the room Mom and Gretch made themselves scarce. Dad approached the side of my bed looking a little apprehensive. He leaned down to give me a kiss and an awkward over-the-bedrail hug. His face showed relief, at last seeing how I looked after the horrible accident. We limited our conversation to pertinent, matter-of-fact details. How was the trip home? Have you had lots of visitors? When do you leave for Mary Free Bed? He only stayed a few minutes because he had to get back to work. After he left I let out a long exhale releasing all the pent up tension and nervousness I felt about our first visit.

The remainder of the day was spent with visitors coming and going. The next day was the move to Grand Rapids to begin my rehabilitation at Mary Free Bed. Instead of feeling frightened about starting rehab, I looked forward to it. Lying in a hospital bed not doing much of anything got really old. I had things to do.

"We choose to go to the moon in this decade and do the other things, not because they are easy, but because they are hard, because that goal will serve to organize and measure the best of our energies and skills, because that challenge is one that we are willing to accept, one we are unwilling to postpone, and one which we intend to win..."

—President John F. Kennedy

CHAPTER FIVE
MISS INDEPENDENT

Arriving at Mary Free Bed and getting settled in was part of a big whirlwind. Gretchen rode up in the ambulance with me. Since she had never ridden in one before, this was pretty exciting for her. What surprised her most was what a bumpy ride it was. Perhaps lying down on a gurney, or having 75 percent of my body paralyzed, gave me a different feel for the ride. I don't remember what any of my ambulance rides felt like. Mom also came up with us, but drove her car behind the ambulance. I remember feeling bummed that, since this was not an emergency situation, we could not turn on the siren and go really fast.

A very nice looking medical student intern did my initial exam to see what (if any) function or sensation I had. The nurses also removed the Foley catheter (a tube inserted into my bladder for drainage into a bag) which I had in since my accident, although a new one had been put in just before leaving Windhoek. The nurses also turned me up on each side to check for pressure sores. Prior to my surgery and stabilizing my spine, the nurses in Windhoek could not turn me for fear of agitating my break. Getting bedsores or pressure sores had not even entered my mind. However, circulation slows and gets cut off to parts of the body if pressure is not relieved. Uncertain about the level of care in an African country, and the long 36-hour trip home, they wanted to see the condition of my skin. I did actually have one red mark on my back from the flight home. Being young and in good health certainly worked to my benefit. Within a day of being turned, the mark faded away.

For the first few days, I had my hospital room to myself. I needed it too, with all the cards and flowers people sent. I had so many cards and flowers—it was quite overwhelming, yet humbling, to see how many people wanted to reach out to me. I had one day to settle in before a full therapy schedule began the next day. The nurses on the floor were wonderful. People come to them because they have lost some major function in life and are nervous, scared and uncertain when first arriving. The friendly nurses warmly greet patients and make them feel comfortable.

My doctor and the medical student intern asked me an array of questions, got out their little pin prick instruments and touched my body at various points. "Can you feel that?" they kept asking as they moved the instrument to various parts of my body. The answer was "No," until they reached my upper torso. The official diagnosis finally came—more than three weeks after my accident. I was a Thoracic 5 Complete Paraplegic. A name and label I had never thought would apply to me.

What amount of function would I have or not have? No one knew the ultimate outcome. I concerned myself with using whatever function I had. My doctor at Mary Free Bed told me that anything that does not come back within one year, will not come back. I did not like that answer. I liked the Namibian, seven-year, philosophy of Dr. Schroeder and Dr.

Opitz better. It is not the role of the doctors and therapists to blow sunshine up their patients' asses about healing and regaining feeling. Their job is to teach patients to live with and function with what ability exists today. And that synced with my thought process. If I ever got something back—great!—if not, I still had to learn how to live with my new reality.

One word appropriately describes my stay at Mary Free Bed: schedule. They do things on a schedule because they have to, but for someone unaccustomed to the rigidity of a schedule, it takes some adapting. Dinner was served at the same time every day, usually around 5:00. The nurses came to get me ready for bed around 8:00 P.M. Granted, I felt tired from therapy and perhaps a bit jet lagged from Namibia, but getting ready for bed at 8:00 P.M. Come on! Then there were the middle of the night visits from the nurses to take blood, turn me or cath me. Even on my first day there, the nurses asked me, "When do you want to shower, in the morning or in the evening?" I said, "You mean I have to decide right now?" Yes, and my decision would stick for my entire stay. They also asked me if I wanted to do my bowel program in the morning or the evening. "My what??" "Bowel program" is the technical term for taking a dump. So many new words, terms, definitions that I *never* would have thought would be part of my life. Here I was, 26 years old and telling the nurse at what time of day I would like to take a shit and have a shower. And the nurse had to know if it would be every day or every other day. With so much to absorb, I got through it by answering one question at a time and moving on to the next thing.

At 2:00 A.M. my first night, two nurses strolled into the room and flicked on the big overhead light so they could measure the circumference of my legs. Not pleased about being awoken from a deep sleep I asked, "Why are you doing this?" One answered, "To monitor the size of your legs to make sure blood clots do not form." They marked my legs so they could measure at the exact location the next time. They would come back a few times a week or weekly to measure the same spots at the same god awful time. Blood still flows in the veins through paralyzed muscles; however the muscles do not contract to push the blood through. Each patient receives blood thinner medication when arriving at Mary Free Bed. It is in the form of a daily shot, so at least I was not able to feel it when they put the needle in my stomach or leg muscle. Gotta be thankful for the small things.

The next day brought my first full day at Mary Free Bed and the nurses got an early start with me. They brought breakfast in first thing around 6:30 and it had to be eaten then. Who wakes up and immediately eats before doing anything else? I never did. After breakfast, it was time to get ready for therapy. Up until this point I had done only some sitting up—and I mean fully sitting up in a chair or in bed. If I had my brace on, I could sit up fully. Without it, I could only sit at a 45-degree angle. To get up and get in the shower, they had to put my brace on me. What truly surprised me was the lightheadedness. It is hard to realize how much the blood drains from your upper body when you sit up and your lower extremities and muscles cannot contract to help pump it back up as fast as it is needed. They got my brace on, got me in the shower chair, and I nearly passed out. They had to keep tilting me backwards to get my legs elevated. Once I felt pretty stable, they took me into the shower room. Wow, did that feel good. I had been bathed and whatnot since my accident, but I had not had an actual shower in close to a month!

To get me dressed, they put me back in bed and pulled out a pair of thigh high TED (anti-embolism) hose compression stockings to put on me. Have you ever seen or felt TED hose? They were thick, inelastic and bright white, not quite like the thigh-high hose one imagines buying at Victoria's Secret. What made putting them on even more challenging was that my legs could offer no resistance or stability when the nurses were pushing against them. Certainly not Victoria's Secret! Then the nurses wrapped a huge white industrial size belly binder around my waist, like you see people on TV wearing to lose weight around their midsection.

Why go through all this? Both items prevent blood and other fluids from collecting in lower extremities. When moving from a horizontal to a sitting position, people with spinal cord injuries can become very lightheaded. To sit me all the way up for the first time in Namibia, the nurses brought me up very slowly so I would not pass out. Again, the paralyzed muscles do not contract to push the blood through the body as they once did. Since therapy started that morning at Mary Free Bed, I would be sitting up for hours. Getting firmly wrapped would minimize the chances of getting light headed and passing out. With my sexy TED hose, belly binder, sweat suit and back brace I felt like I was suiting up for battle rather than getting ready for therapy. However, in a way, this daily ritual became my battle preparation. I prepared to fight to regain some type of normalcy in my life and for every scrap of independence and self-sufficiency I could grasp onto and hold tightly.

When the nurses dressed me, they lifted each leg into the sweat pants and rolled me from side to side to hike them up to my waist. With my brace going on over my clothes, the nurses had to put a shirt on me while I was lying down since I could not yet sit upright without wearing my brace. So they rolled me side to side again to put on my bra and sweatshirt.

Mary Free Bed wastes no time when introducing patients to their rehab routine. The first day I had two Occupational Therapy (OT) and two Physical Therapy (PT) sessions scheduled. Just after I was dressed and still sitting in bed, my OT, Brigit, walked in the room. She was either German or Dutch and spoke with an accent. She was about my age, slender with ear-length brown wavy hair. She introduced herself to me and asked if I had any questions.

With clothes on my mind, I asked, "How am I supposed to try on clothes when I go shopping?" The question surprised her. She furrowed her brow and replied, "I'm not really sure, no one has asked me that before." I looked at her with a you've-got-to-be-kidding expression. She was the "professional!" I possessed no expertise in this area. She was supposed to have all the answers, and she could not answer the first question I asked. OT was off to a smashing start.

Of all the different types of therapy, such as physical, psycho or occupational, I hated OT the most. As I soon discovered, Brigit possessed a great deal of knowledge and patience. I liked her and we got on very well. What made OT so detestable? It focused on daily routine activities. At the ripe young age of 26 I had to re-learn everything. How to dress, shower, put my shoes on and tie them—everything I learned at the ages of three and four! My legs could no longer come up to me to put themselves in my pant leg. I had to figure out a way to move them and put them where they needed to go. And you know what? Legs are HEAVY! The nurses dressed me and did all the lifting for me in the beginning, but I would have to learn to do it all on my own. Dressing by rolling from side to side in bed did not excite me. But I learned and mastered the task because that was the only way I was going to get dressed. It amazed me how much longer it took to do everything. The days of putting on a pair of socks in ten seconds (or less) became a memory.

After the brief introduction, Brigit left and the nurses transferred me from my bed into a wheelchair to go downstairs for my PT. One nurse asked, "Do you want a push to the elevator or do you want to push your own chair?" I replied, "I can go on my own." The nurse directed me to the elevator. Before my accident I had never even sat in a wheelchair, let alone maneuvered and propelled one. This presented a whole new skill set to learn. One tentative push, two pushes with a little more vigor, the chair rolled easily and quietly on the tiled floor. Getting the feel for moving my arms in unison to keep the chair straight, I slowly pushed my way to the elevator. There were a few corners to turn and those went smoothly. Thankfully my chair did not collide with any walls.

Approaching the elevators, I saw others waiting to go to therapy. It felt like being the new kid in school in the middle of the year, trying to weave into and fit in the pre-established patterns. Of the few waiting with me, no one said anything to me; some did not have the capability. In uncomfortable, elevator silence I sat with the group and waited. A moment later the ding from the elevator sounded and the enormous doors parted. An orderly pressed the stop button to hold the doors open, stepped out, greeted us with a friendly "Good Morning" and loaded on people in chairs. The elevator could hold up to four wheelchairs at a time. It was a quiet ride down.

Once off the elevator, I rounded the corner to the therapy gym and a shock jolted through me. Never had I seen so many wheelchairs in one place before—more importantly, wheelchairs with people in them! Momentarily overwhelmed at not only the sight, but the realization that I now belonged to this group, I paused and took a deep breath before continuing toward what looked like Candy Cane Lane, but lined with chairs. No one gave me any specific instruction. It appeared as if patients parked themselves or got parked along the wall and waited for a therapist to find them. No one ever told me exactly what would happen once I arrived downstairs. The experience from my travels taught me not to freak out in new situations. After a few minutes, a tall, friendly woman with very curly, long blonde hair and dressed to the nines approached me and asked, "Are you Jocelyn?" With an internal sigh of relief that someone had come to claim me, I smiled and said, "Yes, that's me." Laurie, my PT for my stay at Mary Free Bed, had found me.

PT became my favorite therapy because it focused on physical gain and improvement. Each morning I started by lifting weights, and the therapists stretched out my legs—the technical term is "range of motion". Building my strength was critical to achieve independence. Men have an advantage over women in that they possess more natural shoulder strength and often progress through therapy faster. At the time of my accident, while not super fit, I was not a fatty either. Rather, I had stayed active and in decent shape. If I faced challenges in adjusting to using a chair with my degree of fitness and youth, those not as healthy or young had an even more difficult time.

In addition to strength building, Laurie and I practiced balance. Since my accident, I had never tried sitting up while unsupported by anyone or anything. With my T-5 injury level, none of my trunk supporting muscles functioned—no back muscles below my point of injury and no abdominal muscles. I had no sense of how much balance I had or did not have. Laurie helped me transfer over to the elevated mat that was at equal height to the cushion of my wheelchair. She kept a hand on me to keep me steady. I perched on the edge of the mat, my feet rested on the floor and my hands were firmly planted on the mat next to my thighs holding me up. Lifting my hands off the mat even the tiniest bit made my heart race and I felt so unstable. Without the support of my arms I could not hold myself up. Imagine trying to balance yourself sitting on an exercise ball without using your legs. You'd feel a bit unsteady. I felt like a Weeble—

those egg shaped toys for kids—"Weebles wobble, but they don't fall down." Well, I could very realistically wobble and certainly fall down. The brace and the belly binder lent some support, but not the support of good 'ol abs. My muscles were weak and nonexistent, but not from lack of use. Rather, neurologically, no signals reached the trunk-supporting muscles to allow them to function. Supporting myself with my hands on either side of me on the mat enabled me to sit up straight, but without that support, I fell right over. We tried playing catch with a ball. I rarely caught the ball because I could not maintain any balance.

After the initial balance exercises, Laurie had me lie on my back on the mat. She took each leg and did a series of movements and stretches with them called range of motion—taking my leg, bending it at the knee, pushing it toward my chin, then straightening it out, raising it up to be perpendicular to the mat and bringing it as close to my chest as possible. It felt like someone was stretching me out to get me ready for a track meet. Some people really tighten up after an accident. Once out of rehab, therapists want patients to continue with their range of motion exercises. Few do and end up with their legs never being able to fully straighten out. I have always been very flexible and the accident did not change that characteristic.

Once range of motion was completed, Laurie helped me sit up. Working on getting to a sitting position when lying down would come in the next few days, but not on day one. Next on the list was weight training. While in the therapy gym, there's no down time. I moved from one thing to the next. As my first full day of therapy concluded, I thought about every new thing I tried or familiar things I tried to do in a new way. In those few moments, I realized how many challenges truly laid before me. How do you prepare yourself for something like this? Rather than wallow in despair and dwell on the difficulty, my attention stayed focused on moving forward and learning all I could to be as independent as possible.

** ** ** ** ** **

For in-patient therapy, Mary Free Bed subscribes to a team approach consisting of one's doctor, social worker, PT, OT, Recreational Therapist and Psychologist. I had a high level of confidence in everyone on my team, except my social worker. We did not really click. She came to my hospital room to introduce herself within the first day or two. A very kind-looking and friendly woman, her appearance offered no foreboding. After a few minutes of chit chat she asked more specific questions about my accident. When I finished, she said, "Too bad this was not a car accident." Out of all the possible things to say in response to hearing my accident story, she chose to point out to me the even bigger downside to my accident. As if paralysis and not walking were not unfortunate enough.

Why would it matter if my injury resulted from a car accident? In the state of Michigan, if you are going to have some type of serious accident or injury—do it in a car accident. Michigan has No Fault auto insurance which includes full medical coverage for any injuries sustained in the accident. This means anything relating to one's accident or injury is 100 percent covered for the rest of the person's life. Any medical supply, procedure or item needed as a result of the accident is covered. No Fault goes far beyond anything traditional medical insurance would cover. Things like assistance with getting and modifying a car or van, modifying a home, additional therapy or specific exercise equipment, attendant care or in-home nursing care after an accident—Michigan auto No Fault covers it all.

My new awareness of Michigan No Fault insurance carried with it some disappointment, but why dwell on it? I needed to work with what I had available to me. She did not need to frequently remind me of it. Nearly every time I saw her she repeated, "Too bad this was not a car accident." I felt like screaming, *SHUT THE HELL UP! I know it wasn't a car accident. Repeating it does not help me.* Anytime a question arose about where I would live after rehab, she would say, "Too bad this wasn't a car accident." As a social worker, I realized she harnessed no magical powers allowing her to say "Alaca-Zam!" to make resources appear which did not exist. However, being ignorant of the social services system, I erroneously believed she possessed a wealth of knowledge of what did exist, and she was simply not sharing the information with me.

Oddly enough, the psychotherapy segment of rehab had the least amount of time devoted to it. I say "oddly enough" because one might think psychotherapy and talking to someone would be most useful after such an enormous, life-altering event. But at that time I did not know what I would have said or talked about. Everything was too new for me. I did not know enough to know what questions I should ask. Being so wrapped up in other rehab therapy sessions did not allow me time to identify and get in touch with my real emotions. Both the nurses and therapists offered to contact some Mary Free Bed spinal cord injury alumni who lead "normal" lives to come and talk to me. But they could only recommend men. No female paras came to mind as good candidates for me to talk to, given injury level, my motivation and personality. I appreciated their offer, but had no desire to talk to anyone—male or female.

I did not feel (or think I was) depressed or have a bad attitude—quite the contrary. What would I have said to the person? Everything was too new. Meeting someone from the other side of the mountain did not interest me. Someday, I would arrive on the other side, but lots of other things had to happen first. One evening while sitting outside Mary Free Bed reading, out of the corner of my eye, I noticed a wheelchair user getting out of his van. He approached me, gave me his card and told me about a Spinal Cord Injury support group that he facilitated at Mary Free Bed which was starting shortly. I politely declined. What I did not say is that I did not want to be around pissers and moaners who complained. With my disability still a novelty, I possessed all my perceptions and assumptions about disability and what a SCI support group would be like. I certainly did not need *that!*

Looking back today on those early months, and even

years, I realize how much depression and anger burrowed deeply into me. I've never been one to outwardly express my emotions or deal with anger well. What do I do with it? How do I express it? But it lurked within me and I rarely let it surface. It mostly appeared in my journal writings, but never in front of others. Despite my adventuresome spirit, love of life and motivation to move on after a life-changing accident, I did, and still do, struggle with depression. However, more on this later. Everyone moves at their own pace on the grief, acceptance and healing road. And the journey is never complete.

Much to my surprise, Recreational Therapy proved to be extremely challenging. Not in the physical sense, because rec therapy consists of dinners, sports and games. Rather, the emotional and psychological part those activities delivered the punch. From the first moment I met Mindy, my rec therapist, I immediately liked her. We talked easily and she asked me about Africa. There were no awkward pauses in the conversation. She was fun, energetic and she made me laugh. Laughter plays an enormous role in the healing process from any traumatic event. The first day, she asked me to start thinking about where I would like to go for a rec therapy trip. The rec therapist at Mary Free Bed would take people out to the movies, dinner, the mall, shopping, just about anyplace to get out of the hospital setting and into the real world setting. This way, patients can gain a sense of the kind of life they *can have* and what *is* possible after acquiring a disability.

Adjusting to life in a chair encompasses many aspects, not

just the physical aspects of learning to maneuver the chair to do certain activities. How others—family, friends, even strangers—see and perceive you plays a monumental role in the transition. The thought of going out in public did not appeal to me. Mary Free Bed was my very safe, sheltered environment. Being in a chair and wearing a big brace did not make me stand out or look drastically different from anyone else in rehab. No one looked at me strangely because I blended into that world. But I did not feel ready to venture outside of my safe harbor. I had traveled around the world by myself, bungee jumped and had many adventures, but I did not yet want to introduce myself to the world as a person with a disability.

My reluctance stemmed from two fears. The first was that going out in public would make my disability more real. Going out to a store or another similar venue I had visited while a walking person might remind me of what life used to be like. I would truly get a sense of what life in a chair would be like. My second fear was people would stare at me because I looked so different. And not look at me in a "whoa, she's a smokin' hot chick" kind of way, but rather in a "what's wrong with her?" freakish kind of way. Like how people look at the homeless guy as he walks down the street, talking to the empty space next to him, wildly gesturing and wearing a winter hat and scarf when it's 85 degrees. Would people now look at me that way?

Every time Mindy saw me, she would ask, "Where do you want to go?" I felt like I was standing on the bungee platform with my ankles firmly bound together, toes hanging over the edge and feeling the weight of the bungee cord dangling below me. Mindy was my counter—the guy who stands next to you and yells, "5-4-3-2-1-Bungee!!!" At the count of 1 you are off the platform and hearing the sound of "Bungee" fade as you free fall. If you do not jump at the count of 1, hesitating makes it harder. With Mindy, I hesitated, and that did not come naturally, especially when it came to physical activities.

Finally Mindy wore me down. About two weeks into my stay, I agreed to leave the comfort of Mary Free Bed. She knew I majored in English and read a lot. She suggested a book store—a local one called Schuler Books and Music. It was a store and café with food and coffee. It sounded like my kind of place. Right from my first rec trip, I got a taste of what an adventure life in a chair can be. Who needs bungee jumping when there is life in a chair?

At this point, my wardrobe still included my brace with the chin and head support. I felt extremely self conscious about how I looked and how other people outside Mary Free Bed would see me. One bonus to this trip was that instead of taking a big Mary Free Bed van—something to make me feel even more conspicuous—we took Mindy's car. She did have nickname for her car—the brown beater. It was a big boat of a car from the 1970's, like a Malibu or Monte Carlo. So between a like-new, clean van with a lift and the brown beater, was I really relieved about riding in the brown beater? Yup.

Mindy pulled her car into the front drive at Mary Free Bed to help me get in the car. I had not yet transferred into a car and Mindy, not being a PT, did not exactly possess stellar transferring technique skills. Getting into the car with a transfer board went off without a hitch. Not necessarily smooth, but successful. A transfer board is a board about eight inches wide and comes in various lengths. One end goes under the bum of the person and the other end sits on the surface to which one is transferring. The board bridges the gap between surfaces. Unfortunately, Mindy did not think to bring it with us. She figured I was small enough that she would have no problem helping me. Ha.

Getting out of the car at Schuler's, however, did not go as smoothly. Still wearing my back brace and not yet having built up much strength in my arms, I provided her little assistance in lifting me. Plus, the car sat lower than the wheelchair. With me in the passenger seat, the wheelchair wedged between the car and the open car door, Mindy did not have a good place to stand to get a firm grip on me to lift me into the wheelchair. Trying to find the best position for her, she backed the chair up a bit, stood at the V where the door hinge is located, reached forward to help me out and up into the wheelchair. Mechanically, it may have worked. However, after the big heave-ho, instead of resting comfortably in the wheelchair, I found myself staring up at the car and Mindy while sitting on the parking lot concrete just in front of the chair. It took so much for Mindy to convince me to go out in public and here we were in the parking lot of the bookstore and she has to lift me off the ground. In imagining what the day would be like, ending up on the pavement never entered my realm of possibility. Disability is like that. Was I upset and emotionally spent? No. When I looked up at her, we both were laughing. This had never happened to her before and I knew she thought, "Oh shit" when she saw me slide to the ground. It was funny. Somehow she got me back in the chair. She really was the perfect person to be with me for that first experience.

Entering the store, I felt very visible, but after a while, picking up books, reading their covers and moving around the store, my apprehension faded away. The store itself had a great feel to it. The bookcases that did not line the walls of the store were all short and light colored, so the store possessed a very open and airy atmosphere. The whole experience was not nearly as bad as I thought it would be. We went to the café, got some coffee and a cookie and chatted a bit. The return trip to Mary Free Bed was smooth. No one ended up on the ground this time. This rec therapy trip took place in May 1997. Of course I did not know it at the time, but five months later in October of 1997, Schuler Books & Music would be my first place of employment as a woman in a chair.

The friend in my adversity I shall always cherish most. I can better trust those who helped to relieve the gloom of my dark hours than those who are so ready to enjoy with me the sunshine of my prosperity.

—Ulysses S. Grant

CHAPTER SIX
THE RIPPLE EFFECT

Stand on the edge of a serene, smooth body of water, hurl in a rock and watch as the stone plunges in, disturbing the tranquility. The jolting impact, the waves spreading far and wide from a single incident: This is how my accident impacted not only my life, but the lives of those around me. While I absorbed the full impact, others felt the ripples as the resonating waves passed by. From thousands of miles away, my friends and family felt the disturbance and rushed to assist in any way they could.

On the night of April 13 in Kalamazoo, after hearing the news of my accident and calling my sister, Mom phoned some close friends to tell them and to ask them to start praying for me. Those who lived in town asked if Mom wanted company or needed them to do anything. Without yet having spoken to Dr. Schroeder and given the late hour, Mom said, "Please just pray for Jocelyn." To some of you, that may not seem like much, but I have come to believe in the wondrous phenomenon of prayer. Those first few phone calls started the domino effect and word of my accident traveled fast.

The following day, after Mom obtained more details about my condition, friends really started to rally. Some came over to be with my mother and assist in making travel arrangements to get Mom on a plane to Namibia. Some of the friends who did not live in Kalamazoo called me at the hospital in Windhoek to offer me encouragement and made sure I knew they kept me in their thoughts and prayers.

Mom had wanted to board the first plane she could to Namibia. However, as mentioned earlier, she did not have a current passport. At one time, both my parents had passports from taking trips to Egypt and Greece, but those trips occurred when Gretchen and I were in elementary school. Being valid for only ten years, their passports expired long ago and Mom never renewed hers. Friends pitched in, calling for flight information, calling the Red Cross (for information on how one returns to the U.S. from a foreign country with a spinal cord injury), and getting a passport in a hurry.

Remember my friend Mary, with whom I was to stay when arriving in Ireland? Mary's mother, Donna, worked for the Red Cross in Kalamazoo. The morning of April 14, the Red Cross received calls about getting a girl back from Africa who had acquired a spinal cord injury. Donna worked all day to find the information, having no idea "the girl" was me. Later in the evening Donna came home and listened to a message on her answering machine from my sister. She listened to it again and again as the news sank in and the shock wore off in learning that I was the injured girl.

Today we take for granted the amount of information available on the internet and the speed at which we obtain it. My accident occurred before the explosion of information instantaneously available on the world wide web and smart phones. Making phone calls, remaining on hold and waiting for responses became the order of the day for everyone helping Mom. Patience became a necessity. At last, someone learned that Mom could get a passport immediately, but would need to drive to the Immigration office in Chicago to apply for one in person. Chicago is about a three-hour drive from Kalamazoo in light traffic. Knowing my mother did not possess her soundest mental state, a friend drove her to Chicago on April 15 to get a passport on the spot.

In the evening on April 14, after the flurry of phone calling subsided, friends who could not be with Mom during the day came over and the group said a Rosary for me. No matter what plans people had earlier in the day or later in the evening, friends put everything aside to lend whatever support they could. Whatever needed to be done, Mom's friends stepped up to assist her in any way they could amidst this sudden tragedy. Sometimes we never discover the impact particular events have on people's lives. Luckily, through keeping in touch and people's willingness to share their experiences, I have become privy to information I ordinarily would never have known.

Some years ago I learned that one of the women in the group, Rosemary, started saying a Rosary every day for me for one year. After the year passed, she kept up her daily ritual, but for other intentions. My accident became a catalyst to reconnect her to an element of her spiritual life that had lain dormant for some time. Another childhood friend of mine, living in Washington D.C. and not a churchgoer, even though she grew up in the Catholic faith, immediately went to church to pray once she discovered what happened. Tragedy can reignite faith and draw people closer. For many of those in my life, faith in God surged to the forefront and suddenly, if only for a short while, became highly important.

When tragedy strikes, people have no idea how they are going to react. How they imagine they would react and how they actually do react could be polar opposites. Prior to my accident, I would have thought losing the use of my legs and being paralyzed would be one of the worst things that could ever happen. But during rehab I discovered this not to be true. The rehab setting proves beneficial in that patients see other patients with a variety of disabilities. I kept saying to myself, *you can always find someone worse off than you.* It helped to stay focused on what I could do rather than focus on all that I lost. Becoming a quad and losing the use of my legs *and* hands would have been worse. Acquiring a brain injury of some sort, even though I may be ambulatory, would be worse. On the flip side, a person with a brain injury or someone missing a limb may look at me and think, "Thank God I don't use a wheelchair."

Oftentimes with a brain injury, the person's personality is never quite the same as before the injury. As my final days at Mary Free Bed approached, one of my dad's co-workers acquired a brain injury from a poor skydiving landing and became a patient at the hospital with me. He made wonderful progress in terms of speech and thought process. To those who had not known him before the accident, he appeared to make nearly a complete recovery. Before his accident, he was animated, outgoing, funny, always quick with a joke and very engaging. Much of it departed forever and no amount of therapy could bring it back. So, given my druthers, I would rather be totally me with paralyzed legs than be walking around and not be me.

Even though I still had full use of my arms and hands, I had to learn how to do everything in a new way. While some tasks presented little or no limitations, like brushing my teeth and hair, the "newness" came from sitting at the sink instead of standing, with very little, if any, trunk support. Instead of leaning over the sink as I brushed my teeth, I now rested my free elbow on the counter to support myself, then filled a cup with water to rinse my mouth. No more leaning over the sink with my mouth close to the running water and quickly moving my toothbrush between my mouth and the running water a couple times to get enough water to rinse out my mouth.

Brushing my hair was really different without the support of trunk muscles. With one hand brushing my hair, the other hand rested on my knee or the counter to help keep me stabilized. And blow drying my hair—another difficult task which requires the use of two hands. I would hold the blow dryer in my left hand and rest my left elbow on the counter and use my right arm holding the brush to style my hair. Talk about learning new skills. Even though I accomplished a lot on my own, at times I needed help. And there were plenty of people around to assist.

All of my good friends from high school came to visit me. Chris, who I had been going to school with since seventh grade, came from Philadelphia just a week or so after I arrived at Mary Free Bed. We went to the same high school and even to the University of Michigan together. Once at college, we rarely saw each other and simply started new lives. Perhaps our junior year in high school had something to do with that.

We had gotten into a fight over a boy. It all blew over and we still hung out together our senior year, but we were just never quite as close as we had been. So it really surprised and touched me that she came all the way to Grand Rapids to see me. It helped me realize that boys will come and go, but your girlfriends, the really good ones, stay forever. Even if they are not physically present.

In talking to Chris in the midst of writing this book, I asked her what she had thought when she heard about my accident and what compelled her to make the trek to Grand Rapids. She said, "I felt so guilty. My long distance friends are important and I am not good at keeping in touch." Sometimes it takes something huge, to realize how dear someone is to us.

As it turns out, I kept many of my close friends from high school. I met people in college and had my group of friends then, but my closest friends, to this day, are those from elementary and high school. We knew each other as children growing into adults before any of us became tainted or jaded by the outside world. These were my "firsts" friends. The first friends to party with, to talk about first kisses, first dates and so many other firsts experienced in those years. We have history. They know me and I them in a way that friends from later in life do not. Being known by someone, not having to put on airs is so deliciously comforting and…real. In a shallow, superficial world I have come to truly appreciate the friends adorning my life.

Another high school friend, Mindy, still lived in Kzoo. I spoke to her on the phone to arrange a time for her to come and visit at Mary Free Bed. We met in fifth grade while taking ice skating lessons. We did not attend the same elementary school or the same college, but we kept in touch. Before our phone conversation ended, she asked, "What do you want me to bring you?" Since my returning to the States, people had brought me so many things—cards, flowers, balloons, plants, a life size cardboard cut out of Rod Stewart. I replied, "Nothing, Mindy. I don't really need anything." But not being one to easily relent on something she really wanted to do, she said, "I'm not talking about what you *need*, I'm talking about what you *want*. You must want something, what about a CD?" Bing! The light bulb went on. With a sigh I replied, "OK, you can bring me *Missing* by Everything But the Girl." She indeed brought it with her. In this age of iPods and Mp3 players, I have the CD to this day.

I have come to realize that people really wanted to help me. In this situation people felt utterly helpless and wanted to do something, almost anything, to feel useful. I have also come to understand that, although they mean well, whatever they do is often a coping mechanism to help them deal with a stressful or scary situation. In this case, no one could do anything to make me walk again. So giving me even the smallest amount of pleasure or comfort during this time was a win-win for both sides. Years later, when talking about our first visit after my accident, Mindy said she was nervous about seeing me. Her anxiety sprang from wondering how I would look. She knew I sounded fine on the phone, but seeing me would be different. When she entered my room, I was lying in bed. Reflecting back on the first moment she saw me, she said, "I was surprised to see you look so normal. I don't know what I thought a paralyzed person would look like, but you looked as if you were just lying down and could hop out of bed at any minute."

I had a steady stream of visitors. Mom came up from Kzoo a few times a week and my sister would drive up with my mother on weekends as well. Plus many visits by good friends in between.

During my first week at Mary Free Bed, Dad did come to visit. Despite my accident and some brief conversations with Dad from the Windhoek hospital, our relationship had not improved and things between us were still pretty tense. I harbored so much anger towards him for his cheating on my mother and leaving the marriage. Even though we were the children—and adult children at that—the divorce devastated Gretch and me too. Regardless at what age it occurs, divorce rips families apart.

The tension between Dad and me seeped into my relationships with my grandparents and my aunt and uncle on his side of the family. My grandparents desperately wanted my sister and me to "forgive and forget" and carry on with Dad as if nothing had happened. In their eyes, we were not being good daughters by remaining angry and distant. However, living three hours away on the east side of the state, they were not the ones sitting next to my mother holding her hand and witnessing her pain and anguish throughout this ordeal. Neither my sister nor I were in a place to make peace with Dad. He did and said very hurtful, manipulative things, to the extent that he became unrecognizable as the father we had known growing up.

My grandparents did not grasp the concept of healing from emotional wounds and the amount of time it can take. They were in their 80's and belonged to a generation that sucked it up through hardships in life and unquestionably did as their elders bid. During my seven-week stay at Mary Free Bed, my grandparents and aunt and uncle, came to see me once. They lived about a three-hour drive away. During my years growing up, given the holidays spent together, the visits and phone conversations with them, I would have received a much higher level of support and encouragement from my dad's side of the family had my parents remained married. It is insights such as this that make the shockwaves of the divorce keenly palpable, recognizing another loss that had not yet become a reality.

Even before leaving for my trip, phone conversations with my grandparents usually centered on my dad and what my sister and I were doing or not doing in relation to him. Shortly after arriving at Mary Free Bed I had a phone conversation with my grandmother. After telling her about my day and my different therapies, I was hoping it would be a light and breezy conversation. When I concluded the therapy recap, a long silence followed. In conversations with Grandma, long pauses did not indicate anything good. A sinking feeling developed in my stomach as I thought, *Oh, no. What is she going to say?*

Before I could interject to steer the conversation to a different topic, she asked, "How come you did not say goodbye to your father before you left for Africa?"

Oh shit, I thought, and bit my tongue. No, I did not make

it a point prior to my departure to contact Dad. He had not showed much respect toward my mom, sister or me over the past few years. I was simply too angry to give him the courtesy of a goodbye call. I replied, "He knew where I was going and when I planned to return. It is not like I left town and never told him anything."

"This happened because you did not say goodbye to your father before you left," she quickly retorted. Feeling like I had been slapped in the face, silently those words sank in. To tell your own granddaughter that she must be being punished for something she did (or did not do). Thankfully I had enough faith, common sense and strength to know she was full of shit. Being raised to not argue with my elders or challenge authority, I made no counter argument. She would believe whatever she wanted to believe. Nothing I said would sway her or change her mind. Since the passing of my grandmother in 2001 and my grandfather in 2002, I have let many things go because holding on did me absolutely no good.

Throughout my parents' ordeal I came to realize how self-centered my dad was. He acted to only serve himself with no regard to how his wife or children might feel about being displaced by another woman and her children. There comes a time in children's lives when their parents suddenly become real people. Almost magically, parents change into people who feel, make mistakes, get hurt and have flaws, just like everyone else on this earth. I first started seeing my parents as real people when I was in college. Being away from home can offer clarity and perspective and remove some of the filters through which we have been seeing our family. But this went beyond seeing my dad as a real person. It was like a high intensity spotlight shining directly on him, revealing nuances and characteristics that those closest to him never knew existed. Or if there were inklings of their existence, my dad was the master of disguise.

So when Dad came to visit me during my first week at Mary Free Bed, things were a bit tense. Aside from my going on this big trip and my accident happening, he knew very little of what was happening in my life. Since he decided to become part of another woman's life and her kids' lives, I felt no inclination to tell him anything about my life. His actions indicated he had no interest in his daughters' lives so why bother telling him anything? At the time I felt too hurt to forgive him. Other than my immediate needs or therapy, we did not have much to discuss.

When setting up the time for our visit, in addition to seeing me, Dad said he wanted to explain some things to me about his actions and why he wanted a divorce from my mom. Allow me to set the stage a bit. At this point I have had a spinal cord injury and been paralyzed for three and a half weeks, been back in the U.S. less than a week, and have *just* begun to realize the amount of work rehab will take and what it means to live in chair for the rest of my life.

In order to stretch out and relax after therapy, I always ate lunch and dinner sitting up in bed from a tray table. Dad came at the end of the day and I was lying in bed talking to him. He pulled a chair close to my bedside to talk to me. Did he ask how I was handling everything? Did he ask about therapy, or even my trip to Africa? No. He did at some point, but not that day. Instead, he started "explaining" why he could no longer be married to Mom and why he went about some things the way he did. He did not apologize or express any remorse for having an affair, distancing himself from my sister and me, or for any of his other behaviors. He said, "Do not judge me. Until you have walked in my shoes, do not judge me. If you were in my place or understood my life, then you would understand why I did what I did."

Silently I listened, stunned. Was he really talking to me about himself? At this point in *my* life, all he can talk about is him? And to talk about walking in his shoes to his paralyzed daughter? Even though he spoke metaphorically, did he even realize what a horrible metaphor it was since I would never be able to walk again—in his shoes or even my own? Part of me could not believe what was coming out of his mouth. Another part thought, *This is typical. Obviously my accident did not change him or make him think differently about making his daughter a priority in his life.* And what I still find remarkable, even today, is he did not see anything wrong with what he said. Or that he spoke only of himself, his needs and what he wanted me to know. What about me, my needs and my new life?

But I never verbalized any of these thoughts to him that day or ever. I just listened. There is a time and place for everything. Certainly this was not the time to begin that conversation, with my lying in the hospital bed, exhausted from a full day of therapy and needing to focus on my adjustment. So, Dad relieved himself of his burden with all he told me, and I listened. I did not intend to completely shut

Dad out of my life, but I was not yet ready to patch things up either. Emotional healing often requires much more time than physical healing. With his busy work schedule, I knew I would not be seeing much of him during my stay at Mary Free Bed, which satisfied me.

While the outpouring response from people truly humbled me, some visits from friends and acquaintances truly surprised me. One unexpected caller was Rob, the guy I dated prior to leaving for Africa. We met when I tended bar at Applebee's. It was 15 minutes to closing one night and he stopped in for a beer or two. We started chatting and he asked for my number. We dated for a few months. I did not take our relationship too seriously because I was stepping out, once again, into the great wide world where anything could happen. I had made my plans before meeting him and saw no reason to change them. Being far less adventurous than I, he could not quite grasp my desire and drive to embark on such a trip. "Why do you want to go to Africa?" he would ask. He produced not one smidgen of enthusiasm when I talked about my upcoming jaunt to Africa, then Ireland. He never said it and probably would not admit it, but I think he wanted me to stay. But my unsettled spirit could not remain grounded. Things officially ended just before I left for my trip.

One day as I returned to my room for lunch, a new roommate had just moved in and was getting settled with her family. As I entered the room, I noticed out of the corner of my eye that someone was standing near my bed. I was still wearing my back brace with the head support, so was unable to turn my head, and I assumed the person was with my roommate. When I got into bed and faced the person, my mouth fell open in shock to see Rob standing there. *How did he even find out?* I wondered. Later, when telling mom about my visitor, she told me her co-worker's husband worked with Rob. Mom wanted him to know what had happened and she wanted to test his character by seeing if he would do anything with the information. When I asked him how he heard, he replied, "My co-worker came up to me and asked, 'Do you know Jocelyn Dettloff?' The first words out of my mouth were, 'She's dead isn't she?'" Given that things did not end well between us, I would say he passed my mom's character test. To arrive unannounced and completely unexpected takes courage, not to mention choosing to see me, rather than merely make a phone call. He visited just once and did not stay long. I have not seen or heard anything from or about him since.

Another shocker came from a phone call one evening out of the blue from Peter—the lovely, sexy Scotsman I met in New Zealand who absolutely knocked my socks off! We lost touch after he went back to Scotland and I returned to the States. At this point I had not heard from him in two years. It was about 8:00 P.M. when he phoned and the nurses were getting me ready for bed. Such is life in the hospital: Your schedule is not your own. The nurses had to finish getting me ready so they could continue with their routine and the other patients. The phone rang and I casually picked it up. The voice I heard on the phone said, "Miss G, this is Peter from Scotland." If I could have jumped for joy, I would have. I could not hide the happiness and elation in my voice. Being that the nurses were not quite finished with me, I said, "I am so happy to hear from you, but could you call me back in 15 minutes, then I'll be able to chat."

The nurses kicked it into high gear as I told them and my roommate about Peter. Even before the 15 minutes were up, he phoned back and the nurses scooted out the door. He first said, in his thick, enticing Scottish brogue, "I was just phoning to say hello and I was thinking it would be nice to see each other again." My heart soared and melted at the same time. With those few words, I discovered I missed the sound of his voice. With hesitation I asked him how he got my number. He said, "I phoned your mum and she gave it to me." Because we had lost touch, Peter is not one of the people who received the dictated letter I had sent from Namibia. Because I had so many overseas friends, Mom gave him my number without saying much or asking any questions. I immediately began to think he did not know anything about my accident. To be sure I asked, "Did my mom tell you where I am right now?" He replied, "No." Oh, shit! This meant I had to drop the bomb. My first few moments of pure joy suddenly turned to dread. I did not want to ruin everything.

After taking one deep breath, without a quiver in my voice I told him where I was and gave him a brief recap of my accident. When I finished, he did not have much to say. He kept repeating, "There's no chance." As if there was no way what he heard was true. But I kept confirming that it did indeed happen. We did not speak for long. Perhaps he needed time for it all to sink in. He said he would ring me back the next evening. The next day passed slowly because I eagerly awaited Peter's phone call later that evening. But he never did phone me again.

Immense disappointment engulfed me. When people would say to me, "You don't want a guy like that anyway." I outwardly concurred, but secretly disagreed. I did want him. I wanted him to ring me back and say it did not matter. I wanted him to come over to the States and visit me. I wanted him to still be captivated by me, despite my using a chair, and fall madly in love with me (again if he had been before). But it did not happen. When his words would have been some external validation that I was still okay, still attractive and still worthy of his interest....I received only silence. This brief experience left a deep wound which took years to heal. And sometimes I question whether I have completely healed from it. Although right then I still had so much to concentrate on in therapy and getting accustomed to using a chair, I had not started thinking much about dating or what that whole part of my life would be like.

Even now I sometimes wonder what became of him. Did he marry? Does he have children? Is he living in his home town, Motherwell, or did he finally move to Australia as he always wanted to do? Through the internet I did find an address for a Peter with his last name in Motherwell. Being somewhat of a risk-taker, I sent him a letter. I never received a reply, nor was my letter returned. I will never know if he received it or whatever happened to him. But you get that as a world traveler. People exit your life just as quickly as they enter.

Looking back on the early days, I am still amazed at people's goodwill and generosity. The woman I saw in Kalamazoo for facials and skin treatments for post adolescent acne came up to Mary Free Bed to give me a treatment. She and my mom scooted the hospital bed away from the wall to allow her to get behind me. She then went to work scrubbing, extracting and buffing away all the impurities of a holiday—sun, sand, booze and poor diet. She did not charge me a penny that day, nor for an entire year of treatments after my accident. She knew I needed a little extra help in getting back on my feet, so to speak.

The most humbling gesture of goodwill and generosity was the fundraiser conducted by my high school, Hackett Catholic Central. Toward the end of my stay at Mary Free Bed, the Hackett Boosters decided to organize a fundraiser and have the proceeds benefit me for anything I may need relating to my accident. The event—a concert—would not take place until October 1997. Prior to the concert, the Boosters sent out a letter, written by my mother, to all Hackett Alumni. She wrote:

It is difficult indeed for me to tell you about my daughter Jocelyn. It is gracious of you to listen. I appreciate this opportunity very much and will try to be as brief as possible. As a 1989 Hackett graduate, Jocelyn Dettloff continued her education at the University of Michigan, graduating in 1993 with a bachelors degree in English Literature. She divided her time between temporary work and extended travel (which was backpacking). Europe, New Zealand and Australia were among her adventures. She was in Africa when her accident occurred.

Her trip began on February 10, [1997] on a truck from Nairobi with a group of 20. They were scheduled to end their trip in Cape Town on April 27. On April 13, Jocelyn was sand boarding (sledding down a sand dune head first) in a park called Soussesvlei, in Namibia which is north of South Africa. Jocelyn's board hit something and she was thrown from it. She landed on her back, broke her Thoracic 5 level vertebrae (just behind her heart) and suffered severe and permanent damage to her spinal cord. Paralysis from her breast down was instantaneous. She waited at the bottom of the dune for 3 1/2 hours until a rescue plane arrived and took her to the capital city of Windhoek.

Jocelyn received excellent medical treatment. Her spine was stabilized with two steel rods surgically inserted on each side. During surgery it was discovered that her spinal cord was still intact, but it was badly stretched and nerves within the cord were severed. She had no head injuries. Jocelyn has complete use of her arms and hands, but because of the location of the injury, she has no feeling or movement in the trunk of her body, legs or feet. We can only imagine what it must be like, at 26, to accept this as reality.

She arrived at Bronson Hospital on May 5, and after two days was taken to Mary Free Bed Hospital in Grand Rapids for rehabilitation. While at Mary Free Bed, Jocelyn did not show any change in her condition. However, she quickly learned all of the tasks and exercises in her physical and occupational therapy classes. It is Jocelyn's goal to live independently. When she was discharged from Mary Free Bed on June 26, she moved into her own apartment in Grand Rapids. She continues her out-patient therapy (three days a week) and is adjusting to her new life and all the challenges it presents. Jocelyn's doctor encourages her to lead an active life, both mentally and physically. He has told *her that if there is going to be a change in her paralysis, it is most likely to happen in this first year. So far....there has been no change...still no feeling and no movement.*

We are hopeful that Jocelyn will find employment when she is ready. There will be a time when her on-going medical costs won't be covered completely and she will have that added burden plus the cost of daily supplies. Jocelyn's wheelchair cost $3,000. The tires on her wheelchair are like bicycle tires and need to be inflated every two weeks. An air compressor would be a big help. Eventually the cushion will have to be replaced...at a cost of $400!

There is much adaptive equipment available to help people with disabilities lead a very full and normal life but all of this equipment is costly. Jocelyn needs a specially designed car. A car would give her more independence, but it will cost around $30,000. Jocelyn attended the Abilities Expo 1997 in Chicago on August 9 and was able (with the help of a Stand-Aid) to stand for the first time since her accident! Such a pleasure to look people straight in the eye and not have to constantly pick up your head to speak to them. That's something you and I take for granted. What a relief to know you may not have to sit in a chair for the rest of your life. The price of a Stand-Aid is $7,200. Participation in numerous sports is still a possibility, but sport chairs cost around $2,000. A special bike is $1,500. Downhill ski equipment starts at around $2,000. With your help these are some of the things that would bring Jocelyn greater freedom and more independence.

There is a possibility that Jocelyn will be able to participate in a Para-Step program. Para-Step is walking with electronic braces *with the help of a walker. It is an extremely difficult program and becomes even more difficult for Jocelyn because of her loss of balance in the trunk area of her body. It does not mean she will be free of her wheelchair. It is another option for standing and perhaps walking (not as you and I walk) but at a very slow pace. The Para-Step program costs. $22,000.*

One cannot begin to imagine the total medical, physical, mental, and emotional cost of this accident. One cannot put a price tag on quality of life and one cannot buy happiness. I can tell you I would rather not be writing this letter. We all grieve her loss and hope she will find some measure of contentment and joy in the future. Thank you for your interest and please pray for Jocelyn.

    With hope,
    Sharron Dettloff

Along with the letter came the announcement for a concert at the Hackett gymnasium with Domestic Problems performing, a local band with a Blues Traveler/Bare Naked Ladies sound. The lead singer, Andy, was one year younger than I. We attended the same elementary and high school and had attended school together since second grade. His band started during his college days at Aquinas College in Grand Rapids. The band agreed to play pro bono and donate all ticket sales and other contributions that evening to me. The mailing and concert together raised a total of $26,000!! For me! The generosity stunned me. The money raised was put into a special fund to assist with injury-related items, services and expenses.

There is no doubt about it, using a chair keeps me humble. As an independent, do-it-myself woman, asking for help did not and does not come naturally. Part of the American persona is being strong, independent, not needing help and overcoming obstacles on one's own. I never wanted people to see me as weak. Advertisers, media and Hollywood have succeeded in creating the illusion of what it means to "be happy," "be successful," and "have it all." The illusion stifles imperfection and weakness. When you no longer have control over your own body; when some tasks become physically impossible to do; when you are forced to ask for assistance—*knowing* the illusion is a sham is one thing, *living* amidst the shards of the shattered illusion is an entirely different beast.

My accident drove home the reality of how much I do *not* have control over in my life. Not only in relation to life's events like meeting my spouse, a flight being delayed or running into someone by chance, but no longer having control of my body, bladder or bowels. I was thrust into completely uncharted territory. Everything—getting dressed, putting on shoes, going to the bathroom, preparing meals— took so much longer, which annoyed me immensely. Gone were the days of jumping out of bed and getting ready in 20 minutes. Through routine and lots of practice most tasks are much faster, but getting ready in the morning is down to as fast as it is going to get. A spectacular day would be getting ready in an hour, but from rising to out the door is usually an hour and fifteen minutes to an hour and a half.

To keep my annoyance level at a minimum, I try to focus on the positive and be thankful for small things, like making all the green lights on the way to work or finding a good parking spot downtown. It is humbling to look for the good things, especially on those bad days when nothing seems to go smoothly. If I fall out of my chair when I'm alone, I'm thankful for the ability to get back into my chair myself. If I spill red wine on my white carpet, I am thankful for being able to clean it up myself. If my wheel rolls away from me while getting into the car, thankfully somehow, someone is always nearby to retrieve it. "My little angels" I call them who happen to be right there when I really need someone. Because I can no longer do everything for myself as I once did, ironically, asking for assistance has allowed me to be more independent. It also made me realize that it is OK to ask for help, that people in our culture do not ask for help enough and that we have lost something in not relying on other people.

"We must be willing to get rid of the life we've planned, so as to have the life that is waiting for us. The old skin has to be shed before the new one can come."

—Joseph Campbell

At the time of my accident, I would have classified myself as active and moderately fit, despite all the good African beer recently consumed. Even as a reasonably fit person, rehab and strength building were damn hard work. As a woman, I lacked natural shoulder strength that men typically have. Yet again, men declare another advantage over women. Typically a male para leaves rehab sooner than a female para because the woman needs more time to build up strength. Lifting weights every day, learning to lift myself from the bed to the chair and lifting myself up in my chair (the technical term is pressure relief) for 10+ seconds all assisted in strength building.

With much practice, I mastered my daily living activities— getting out of bed, getting dressed, taking a shower, preparing food in the kitchen and exercising…all with wearing my lovely brace. I eagerly awaited the day to be unencumbered by it. When tasks proved difficult or awkward my therapists said, "It will be different when you get your brace off." The brace finally came off for about the last two weeks of my stay. Unfortunately, things were not as different as I hoped. The upside was no more rubbing on my chin from the head support, and I could turn my head. The downside was my balance still sucked and I still had to hold myself upright using my arms most of the time. The brace at least helped with providing my core and trunk with some support. However, once removed I felt even more unstable. Imagine standing on a balance ball—a ball with a little disk platform around the circumference to stand on. People tip, sway and flounder until they find their balance point. Trying to sit up without a brace, with only my hands supporting me or something to lean against, was like that; except I never found my balance point, even to this day.

In the midst of getting reacquainted with the way my body worked and relearning to do everything in the sheltered environment of the hospital, the real world started knocking at my door. As if the physical loss and limitations were not enough to occupy my time, soon the social worker began posing the questions Where will you live when you leave? What will you do for income? Will you have insurance? I could not answer her because I did not even know my options or what resources existed.

I knew nothing about public assistance programs. When not reminding me that it was too bad my injury was not from a car accident, the social worker did prove useful in applying for benefits. As a person with a medically documented disability I would be eligible for Social Security Disability Income (SSDI which is based on work history). She helped me apply for SSDI, Medicaid and temporary Social Security Income (SSI which is assistance without a work history)—a necessity until my SSDI became approved. Talk about places people think they will never visit in their lifetimes. Here I am, a college graduate, world traveler, industrious wage-earner, applying for public assistance programs. Me?? Was this really my life? Indeed.

As I progressed through therapy and met the goals my therapists set for me, the insurance company, naturally, wanted me discharged as soon as possible. I had been at Mary Free Bed for over six weeks. Yep, life and all physical function completely changes, and insurance companies expect you to just bounce back. As time goes on, rehab stays get shorter and shorter.

Now that financial assistance paperwork was filed, the next big question—Where am I going to live?—hovered over me. Part of rehab therapy is getting back into one's regular environment. I received day passes to go to the mall with friends or family and even an overnight pass to go back home to Kalamazoo. There were few options for where I'd live when getting out of Mary Free Bed. My staying one night in Kalamazoo at my mother's house immediately ruled out her home as a potential residence. Features like three steps up to the house, a half bath on the main level and no bedroom on the main level made the house impossible as a residence. This is when we began to learn about what health insurance does and does not cover. A ramp, for instance, to get in and out of the house is not considered a medical necessity. My sister's house presented even more obstacles, and living with Dad was not on my radar screen.

What about living in Grand Rapids? Before leaving for my trip, I knew that once I returned from Ireland I wanted to give living on my own a go. In previous years I had always lived with roommates in college, after college, while traveling and then with Mom. I had never had my own place. Even with my accident, I saw no reason to alter my dream. And

I still felt no desire to live in Kzoo. But where would I live in Grand Rapids? My supplemental income would last until my SSDI became approved, but that would be only $254.00 a month! How was I supposed to live on that? I needed to find a wheelchair-accessible, subsidized apartment—and fast. The end of June was approaching and the insurance company wanted me discharged the first week of July. With a subsidized apartment, I would pay 30 percent of my income for rent and Housing and Urban Development (HUD) would make up the difference. Paying 30 percent of my $254.00 income left me with only $176 each month for the rest of my living expenses—food, transportation, phone, etc...How would it all work? Well, somehow it had to.

In addition to the question of where to live, the issue of transportation reared its ugly head. How would I get around Grand Rapids and to my out-patient therapy sessions? With selling my car before my trip and spending all my money on my trip, at this point, I had no money to buy a car. A paratransit system called Go!Bus solved my problem. Areas offering a public transportation system, by federal law, also have to offer a paratransit system which will take seniors and persons with disabilities from their door to their desired location. Oftentimes the public transit stop is too far from one's home or the mainline bus and subway system are simply not accessible. Go!Bus riders needed to apply and be approved for this service. At the time, the fee per ride was $2.50 or $5.00 round trip.

With my discharge date staring me in the face, a barrier-free, subsidized apartment became available at the end of

June. I felt excited to leave the hospital, but nervous about moving full time into the real world. Not to mention moving somewhere new without knowing a soul. I reflected back over my life to pinpoint the last time I moved somewhere completely new alone. The answer—never. As a child moving from Toledo, Ohio to Kalamazoo, Michigan my family was with me. When going to college, nine other classmates from high school also went to the University of Michigan and of those nine, five were friends. Plus, my sister had one more year of college there when I started. Even on some of my travels, I may not have known anyone starting the trips, but I knew I would meet people. However, a trip was a temporary time period, nothing like moving to a different city and starting over from scratch.

On Thursday, July 3, 1997, less than three months after my accident and just before Independence Day, Mary Free Bed discharged me. Thankfully, Gretchen and Tim helped move me and outfit my apartment with some of their old furniture. Mom stayed with me for a few days to get me unpacked, settled and organized. Having people do so much for me was humbling and made me so grateful. Even though it drives me nuts sometimes, I do appreciate having the organization queen as my mother.

Remaining in Grand Rapids was certainly the right decision. I love my mother dearly and could not have progressed as well without her love and support. However, living an hour away from her and the rest of my family forced me to become independent. Not only did I take on all the duties required for living alone—the cleaning, laundry, shopping—they were all done using a wheelchair. If I wanted to go to therapy, to eat or to vacuum...whatever, I needed to figure out a way to do it. Without friends or family close by, I had no one to call to "come over real quick" to help me out. Living far from my family also forced them to let me become independent. Had they lived close, whether in Kalamazoo or Grand Rapids, Mom, bless her, would have been over at my place nearly every day, especially at the beginning, checking in and making sure I did not need anything. In those early days, the stubborn three-year-old child in me reared her head more than once if Mom tried to help me when I did not want help. Her staying with me for a few days in my new apartment sufficed.

I liked my new two-bedroom place. At first glance, the apartment did not look much different from any other apartment, even though it was designed for people with disabilities (universal design). Features which made the unit universally designed included an open floor plan with the only separate rooms being the bedrooms and bathroom, zero step (no step) entrances at each door of the building, carpeted main hallways and bedrooms without plush padding, lever handles instead of door knobs so those with little or no hand strength could open a door by using a fist or an elbow, linoleum flooring in high traffic areas instead of carpet, kitchen counters at 34 inches rather than the standard 36 inches. The sinks in the kitchen and bathroom had cutouts underneath so a wheelchair user could get close to the sink, and the huge bathroom had a large roll-in shower instead of a bathtub so an entire wheelchair could fit into the shower—

not a person's everyday wheelchair, but a plastic and padded chair designed for the shower.

The night after Mom left would be the first night spent completely by myself in, quite truthfully, years. Being in Australia and New Zealand, people were always around; the year in Kzoo I lived with Mom; in Africa I had a tent mate or roommate the entire time; in the various hospitals, if I did not have a roommate, pressing a button sent a nurse right in. I spent no time thinking about this on that night or that it was my first night alone as a paralyzed person. The pleasure and satisfaction of finally having my own place fully occupied my thoughts.

To relax and watch TV after the day of cleaning and organizing, I wanted to get out of my chair and sit on the couch. I was not yet very good at transfers without a transfer board. Pulling up to the couch I assessed the height difference and distance between my wheelchair and the couch cushion. It looked pretty even. Deciding it would be an easy transfer, I did not get a transfer board and situated my chair at (what I thought) would be a good angle to swing my bottom onto the couch. It seems bad decisions always make the best stories. Aloud I counted, "1, 2, 3, lift." With one fist on the couch and one fist on my chair, something went haywire and instead of swinging onto the couch, I sank right to the floor. Shit! At this point my arms were getting stronger, but overall were still on the weak side. My mother was an hour away and I had not yet learned how to get from the floor back into my chair. At that moment I realized using a chair forces one to become a creative problem solver.

What did I do? I took one of the cushions from the couch, put that next to me on the floor, lifted myself up onto that cushion, dragged and clawed myself up onto the cushionless side of the couch, bumped myself up onto the side with the cushion and then managed to get back into my chair. All while remaining calm and not panicking. My arms tingled and felt like jelly. This was the hardest workout they had ever had. With my hands slightly quivering, I picked up the phone to call my mommy. When she answered, I burst into tears, not from being physically hurt in any way, just frustrated that this is now my life. So she would not panic when hearing my tearful voice, right away I said, "I'm fine, but..." and told her what happened.

Another lesson in humility. But as with any unpleasant experience, I learned from it, put it behind me and moved on. Mom offered some words of comfort and said she was proud of me for coming such a long way in a short period of time. After we hung up, I tried the transfer again without a board and landed on the couch successfully.

Moving into my own place after being discharged from Mary Free Bed absolutely amazed people. But to me it felt like the most natural thing to do since that had been the plan after returning from Ireland. Having a major function in life taken away from me and using a chair did not squelch the desire to live by myself and did not become a barrier. What people consider impressive or inspiring, I consider mundane tasks needed to be done to live life. It ultimately boiled down to making decisions, consciously or subconsciously. But make no mistake, my MO carried with it much internal struggle. More on this later.

People often viewed me as strong, having a good head on my shoulders and independent. Even one of my high school teachers called me feisty. When my accident happened, many said, "You're a strong person. If this had to happen to someone, you're a good person to have it happen to." How does one respond to that?! Just as people have feelings of helplessness, they also struggle with finding something meaningful, insightful and comforting to say. But when analyzing those comments, I think, *Would it be better to be a weak sapling walking than a strong person rolling?* If I were a sapling, it would not feel natural and certainly not be me. And what a tragic loss for the world to not have the feisty, strong-willed me. I know people were trying to convey something positive and good. Those comments did not anger me; instead they made me realize how many people had a far better sense for who I was than I did.

September of 1997 rolled around and I found myself well settled in my new digs. I still went to Mary Free Bed a few days a week for out-patient therapy, but that would soon wrap up. I began to think about getting a part time job. My SSDI benefits would likely be approved, but I did not want to sit around and get bored, especially with fall around the corner, and the long Michigan winter not far behind. For employment, I did have some contact with the local state-run vocational rehabilitation office—a state organization to assist people with disabilities in finding and obtaining work. I did not find them to be particularly helpful. The sorts of jobs they tended to find for people with disabilities were store greeter type jobs. They suggested a job as a receptionist, but I sought something more active and challenging. I would not have applied for a job as a greeter prior to my chair, why would I now?

I talked to my rec therapist, Mindy, about getting a part-time job, She suggested that a bookstore or other stores may be looking to hire Christmas help soon. With Schuler Books & Music being the only bookstore I had visited in Grand Rapids, I phoned them to see if they were hiring for Christmas. Sure enough, they were. Since my only mode of transportation was Go!Bus, the paratransit system, I asked the store manager if we could set up a time for me to come in, fill out the application and do an interview all at once. He said that would be fine. A few days later, I applied for my first job as a person using a chair.

Even before leaving my apartment, I convinced myself this place would never hire me because of my wheelchair. Entering Schuler's, I approached the information desk and asked for Jeff, the manager with whom I had spoken. Jeff, a quiet, slight man with glasses and salt and pepper hair (a bit more pepper than salt), came to the desk, greeted me, handed me the application and suggested filling it out in the café. As if applying for the job were not intimidating enough, the application surprised me. The store was divided into two sections—books and music. Applicants could specify if they wanted to work on the book side, the music side or both. Then, based on one's choice, there were two daunting quiz sections for books and one section for music. Checking the "Book" box, I proceeded to the first intimidating quiz. Listed before me were 30 plus authors, historical figures and other well-known (or rather, should be well-known if working in a bookstore) people. The task was to fill in what section of the bookstore the name would be found. For example, Agatha Christie—Mystery, Nora Roberts—Romance, James Joyce—Fiction. You get the idea. However, the names actually on the application were not that easy. I fared much better on the next section. Here 25-plus book or poem titles were listed and I had to name the author or poet, such as, *The Color Purple*—Alice Walker, *Catch 22*—Joseph Heller, *Alfred J. Prufrock*—T.S. Eliot. This is one of the few times being an English major came in very handy and I could put my outstanding U of M education to work.

As if handing in a quiz for a grade, I reviewed all blank questions on the application to see if any more could be answered correctly. With the application completed as thoroughly as possible, I capped my pen, set the application on my lap and pushed back to the information desk. When I handed the application to Jeff, he looked it over and we walked back to the cafe for an interview. I was so nervous. It had been well over a year since my last job interview of any kind, let alone one as a chair user. As I had learned from the very beginning, the task to make others feel comfortable fell upon me. I knew what Schuler's was seeking—temporary help for the Christmas season, October to January. Without knowing the legal do's and don'ts of what people with disabilities should/should not say in an interview or what employers can/cannot ask during an interview, I went purely on instinct.

Instinct told me people are curious. If I were the person

meeting me, I would be dying to know why this young, vibrant person used a wheelchair. Having a tendency to be rather direct, as the interview got underway, I told Jeff about my accident and my intention to find part-time employment of no more than 20 hours per week. Aside from my therapy sessions, I would be available at any time, any day of the week. Jeff was a friendly, yet very reserved, person. I did not get any sense of the interview going particularly well or particularly bad. In my opinion, it went fine, but his not hiring me because of my using a chair kept creeping into my head.

The interview concluded. He said he would let me know in a few days. I looked around the store for a bit until my Go!Bus arrived to take me home. Later the very same day, Jeff called to offer me a job. Wanting to sound semi-professional, I struggled to control my overwhelming joy while speaking to Jeff. If I could have done a cartwheel, I would have. Feeling elated, relieved and impressed that an employer looked beyond my chair and saw the skills I had to offer, I called Mom to tell her the good news.

In October 1997, six months after my accident, I commenced working as a book seller. Not as a greeter or some comparable position, but as a book seller with all the same duties as any other employee. Well, all the same duties except for shoveling snow from the front walk during the winter. I rotated around to different information desks, the register, and even had my own section to shelve and straighten—Crafts and Home Construction. Looking back on the interview, I now understand that Schuler's sought particular types of people for the store environment. Despite my own insecurities and thinking, *They're never going to hire me because of my chair,* I realize I fit what they sought, and just happened to use a chair. Schuler's housed a very eclectic and open-minded staff. I could not have orchestrated a more ideal place for me to continue adjusting to my new reality. This job was a perfect first job as a person using a chair. It exposed me to many different kinds of people, both co-workers and patrons, and it exposed many people to me—a person with a disability doing all the same work—shelving, the information desk, the registers—as those without disabilities.

"There are two tragedies in this world, not getting what one wants and getting it."

—Oscar Wilde

CHAPTER EIGHT
FROM INVINCIBLE TO INVISIBLE

What is the number one demographic group to sustain a Spinal Cord Injury (SCI)? Males 18 to 25 years old. Two words sum it up—high risk. Members of that demographic pay higher car insurance premiums. They have a reputation for taking more risks and many opportunities to participate in extreme sports. They possess an undaunted sense of self which leads them to think nothing can harm them. Women in the same age group also participate in some of the high-risk activities of their male counterparts, but not in the same large numbers. When I traveled, thrill seeking was IT! Rarely did stories of accident or tragedies surface about bungee jumping, skydiving or white water rafting. If one does not hear the stories, then one considers it safe enough to do. Cloaked in my sense of invincibility I thought if other people participate in activities and do not sustain injuries, why would I?

When in New Zealand, I actually did some hitchhiking by myself. Yes, a totally taboo activity here in the US, especially by a lone female. On North Island I hitchhiked from Taupo down to Wellington about 200 miles (315 kilometers), then back up to Taupo. A few weeks before my solo attempt, a story hit the news about a driver who picked up a hitchhiker and then was robbed and beaten by the hiker. Did that change my mind about hitchhiking? Heck no. No harm came to the hitchhiker, so why would any harm come to me? If the roles were reversed and the hitch hiker was harmed, I would have found alternative transport to Wellington. In Australia, the thought of hitchhiking did not enter my mind because of too many occurrences of hitchhikers being robbed, beaten and killed. Back in 1995, New Zealand still fell in the "safe" category.

When staying in Queenstown, New Zealand, on the day before my twenty-fourth birthday, Barb and some others planned on motorcycling for the day. Not knowing how to ride a motorcycle and thinking that day was not the time to learn, I passed on going along. As I prepared my breakfast in the backpacker's kitchen, a Canadian physics professor from Vancouver staying at our hostel walked into the room and asked if I wanted to go mountain biking. Hmmm…a manual mountain bike I could handle. Plus, he was in his late 20's, tall, fit, had wavy chestnut hair with lightened sun-kissed swirls, a bronze glow to his skin and absolutely lovely. As an English major, I never cared much for science, but if he had taught at my university, I would have majored in physics.

He quickly explained he and a photographer for Avanti bikes were heading to Skippers Canyon and they needed another person to be in the shots. It sounded right up my alley. I had ridden a mountain bike plenty of times, but had never done any off-road riding. How hard could it be? Considering the offer for perhaps one nanosecond, I seized the opportunity. With everyone else gone, my own little adventure for the day had sought me out. I quickly finished eating. The photographer picked us up at the hostel in a van with the bikes and we headed to Skippers Canyon.

Once at the canyon and suited with bikes and helmets, the professor, who obviously had done this a few times before, tore off down the trail. The photographer jogged ahead of the professor to suss out the shots he wanted. This left me to figure out off road riding by myself. I quickly discovered when going down steep hills that one should not use both the front and rear brakes simultaneously. This causes the bike to slide sideways. When riding on a trail about two feet wide with a rocky hill on the right and a plunging cliff on the left, sliding sideways is not something I wanted to do.

After my first time falling off the bike, I sprung up unscathed, determined to master this off-roading business. The second fall proved a bit more dangerous, but essentially I remounted the bike unscathed. However, eyeing the trail's steep descent in front of me, nervousness crept in. But I had to catch up with the other two, so I climbed on the bike again and started to slide. Before it happened, intuition told me I would fall. Like an out of body experience, I watched it all take place in slow motion, being powerless to stop the pull of gravity. As the bike started to slide, I looked over the cliff to see where I would land, and said "Oh shit!". Luckily I did not fall terribly far, but did land in the middle of a bush with inch-long thorns.

There I lay, on my back on the thorn bush with my bike on top of me. Other than the thorns poking me in the ass and thighs, I felt no other pain and sustained no injuries. *How am I going to get out of this one?* I thought. To get leverage to lift myself, I had to push down on something, but only inch long thorns were beneath me. So, the McGuyver in me leapt into action. I lifted the bike off me, put it to my side, took off my helmet, put it under my hand and pushed down on the helmet for leverage. At that point I could then get my other hand on the bike to push myself up and climb out of the bush. Just as I started to ascend back to the trail, the two guys came back up the path looking for me, happy to see me not too beat up. I had a few nice scratches on my limbs and my ass looked like a strawberry for a week. Happy Birthday to me!

** ** ** ** ** **

As easy as I made my adjustment look, a sneak peek on the inside revealed a completely different reality. There are things I miss terribly, aside from the obvious, like walking and having sensation. Every spring I get the urge to run. Maybe it is because I ran track in high school and associate spring with running. Maybe it is seeing people crawl out of hibernation and get outside. But the urge certainly is strongest in the spring.

I miss doing things in the same manner as before. Now, I do most of what I did before, just differently. There is not one thing that I do that is the same as before being in a chair, mainly because of my balance. Yes, I can still brush my hair, put on makeup, brush my teeth relatively the same, but now I'm always leaning on the counter or have my back against something to hold myself up and free up a hand. Plus I always have to be ready for a muscle spasm to throw me off balance. Many people with spinal cord injuries get muscle spasms. Muscles below the point of injury still send signals to fire. In a non-injured spinal cord, the signal travels up the cord to the brain and the brain then allows or prohibits the muscle from moving. With a break in the spinal cord, the signal travels to the injured point and back to the muscle again. Movement, like taking my foot off my footplate or getting into the car, typically sets off a spasm. Other times, a spasm catches me completely by surprise. My spasms are not painful, just annoying at times. Luckily I have quick reflexes and can grab onto things in a hurry to catch myself. Even tasks like putting on shoes are different because I have to lift my feet and bring them up to my lap to put on my shoes.

In the summer of 2004 I was reminded of just how great balance is. While putting something away underneath my kitchen counter I had my hands full and was not hanging on to the counter. I started to fall forward and lost my balance. With no spare hands available to grab my chair or the counter to stop myself, I plunged head first into the counter. I cut my forehead open just a bit, not bad enough for stitches. Being alone, I'm lucky I did not knock myself out and fall out of my chair. In these bad situations, I find that I look for the good and how it could have been so much worse.

While adjusting well to using a chair and learning to live with my current circumstances, some things will never be completely okay and I will probably miss them for the rest of my life, sometimes more, sometimes less. I still remember what it feels like to stand on the edge of a step, balance on the balls of my feet, raise myself up onto my toes and feel the tightness crawl up my calves. Then, slowly lower myself, allowing my heels to dip below the step, savoring the deep stretch and release in my calves. I wonder if I will ever forget this sensation. I hope not. Just like any good memory from my past, I want to hang on to it. But it does make me miss being able to do it.

One incredible difference I've noticed between pre and post chair is people assume I need help. They often offer to assist me and I politely decline. The operative word there is politely. Perhaps the person had never asked a person with a disability if he/she needed assistance. If I snap at the person or reply rudely, the person will probably have no inclination to offer assistance to another person with a disability ever again. Once, when Mom and I were shopping, she went into the restroom and I waited outside the door with all our bags. Someone approached me and asked if I needed help and I said no. Now, had I been standing there with all my packages, it is highly unlikely anyone would have asked if I needed help. Because I am so independent, I often assume people think I just can't do it, and perhaps my assumption is incorrect at times.

People tend to take for granted the smallest, seemingly insignificant things. No one thinks about the challenges that exist until in the situation themselves or hanging out with me. A challenge most people do not think about is the physical space created around me because of the chair. Think about greeting friends, family and acquaintances. You walk up, give them a hug, put your arm around them or shake their hand. Your personal spaces briefly intermingle through physical contact or standing close together. When using a mobility device like a walker, cane or wheelchair, it is not easy to get close to people and give them a hug or touch them as it used to be, and the reverse is true too. Any mobility device acts as an extension of a person's body. So, while the walker or wheelchair may be intermingling with another's personal space by being in close proximity to others, the *person* using the mobility device does not always feel the closeness. As a result, it is harder to get physically close to people and ultimately emotionally closer too.

This reminds me of a weekend Bible study retreat with a group I knew well and was very involved with. We carpooled and caravanned going to the out of town retreat. On the return trip, all the drivers (of which I was one) caravanned back to the carpool site to drop people off at their cars. People said their goodbyes, giving each other hugs, but only a few people came to my car to say goodbye to me and that was after one of the girls said, "Don't forget to say goodbye to Jocelyn." And when they came up to say goodbye, it just was not the same as being able to stand up and give them a hug like everyone else.

On a different retreat, we had a free afternoon for people to go out and play football, go on a hike or just hang around the retreat lodge. Had I not been in a chair, the hike would have been my first choice, but since hiking was not an option, I knew I'd be hanging around the lodge. And for the first time (and this was at least five years after my accident) it really bothered me that I could not do what I wanted or what the majority of my friends were doing. It put me in a foul mood. A bunch of women were using the bathroom before the hike and I was in the bathroom as well. One woman asked me, "Are you going on the hike?" The "Duh, what-do-you-think?" look on my face must have said it all. When she looked at me for my answer, she felt silly for even asking the question. However, it goes to show that she did not think of me as a chair user, she simply saw me as my adventurous self and naturally thought I'd want to go on the hike.

Dating presents challenges for anyone. However, dating is more challenging for people with disabilities, especially women with disabilities. I am single and do want to marry and have a family. It surprises me the number of people, even some friends, who assumed that since I used a chair I would also want a partner who used a chair. Heck no! Over the years, I have discovered one disability is hard enough. I have dated both able-bodied men and men who use chairs. I prefer able-bodied men who can piggyback me up a flight of stairs. Being light enough and willing enough to be schlepped around allows me to go more places and do more things. I typically respond to people saying, "If one wears glasses, do you assume they only want to date someone with glasses? Or if one has brown hair they only want to date brown-haired people?" Their response is always no. When I verbalize those questions, people realize the ignorance of their assumption.

Looking back on my high school and college days, I consider myself a late bloomer. During college I studied a lot and did not date anyone even though I wanted to date and have a boyfriend. I was always the cool chick to hang out with, but never the woman that men beat down the door to date. Back then I did not exhibit the self-confidence I have today. At least now I consider myself to be attractive and can assuredly say what I like about me, whereas back then I could not have. My illogical thought process went something like *men ask out attractive women. Men did not ask me out or show an interest in dating me, ergo I must not be attractive.* Regardless of how ludicrous it sounds, it made perfect sense to me at the time.

Traveling helped me reveal a side I kept hidden. More of the Zsa Zsa G'Jocelyn and Miss Maude Hotcycle who buried herself ages ago after moving to Kalamazoo. During college, I did not want to disappoint my parents because their money paid for my education. Traveling, however, was on my dime. I felt more freedom to do what I wanted rather than what someone else wanted me to do. At some point I had to declare my life my own. When returning to the states after New Zealand, I started receiving more attention from men and dating a bit. I never felt I possessed the feminine wiles or flirting skills some of my other friends manifested.

Just as I started exploring the dating and relationship world, my accident brought it to a screeching halt. As I dipped my toe into my later twenties and began feeling more comfortable with myself as a person and my appearance, now this wrench—a really fucking big wrench—got thrown into the mix. Looking in the mirror, I think I'm attractive. My mother and others (sometimes friends, sometimes strangers) tell me, "You're a beautiful girl." But internally I push back and resist accepting what they say as truth. I wonder, *What do single men my age think when they see me? Do they see ME at all? Do they only see an object with some wheels but no person?*

Once, years ago, while playing wheelchair tennis, I arrived at the tennis club for one of our team's indoor, winter practices. To reach the tennis courts, we passed through the weight lifting area. Cruising through I noticed, as I often did, the many very fine looking men working out. I also spotted a few women in the mix working out in their little spandex outfits. Then, like a ceiling tile crashing down upon me, a dating theory revelation struck me. My revelation told me men are very (okay extremely) visual. Typically, their idea of "beauty" does not incorporate a wheelchair or any other sort of disability. Men, especially those in their later twenties and early thirties, tend to see the chair and only the chair before they notice the person using the chair. Even if men saw the woman using the chair, initially, they are not likely to see her as dating potential. When a guy notices a feature on a woman it is usually something like her "rack" or her ass. Rarely is it, "she had a great personality, a great smile or a great sense of humor."

Men in chairs, especially athletes, face a different reality. Just to confirm my theory, I spoke to a few single guys with whom I play tennis who use chairs. Both these guys are good looking, athletic and fashionable. And they live in different cities, one in Grand Rapids, the other in Northern Michigan. When either of them goes out to a bar, they have no problem meeting women. In fact, women come up and start talking to them! The men on my wheelchair tennis team who are married and/or attached all have able-bodied partners. None of them has a partner with a visible disability and, to my knowledge, not a hidden disability either.

Women are much more nurturing and less visual than men. Women tend to see beyond the chair and see the good-looking guy. When asked what feature she notices on a guy, a woman is more likely to say "his eyes, his smile or his great sense of humor." A guy in a chair appears less threatening to women which makes her more confident to chat him up. Plus, a woman can sit in a guy's lap and it's sexy and fun. The reverse does not look too sexy or cool for either person. Men like to appear confident and skillful; they do not like looking foolish. No one relishes looking foolish; however, a woman is less likely to mind looking silly than a man.

Take dancing for example. Dance floors are packed with women and the majority of men will only venture out after having a few drinks under their belts. Why? Because, when sober, men typically are too insecure about how their dancing skills (or lack thereof) may look to others. From a very early age, I have told my nephews that girls like boys who can dance! A woman in a wheelchair can produce the same insecurities in men. They do not want to look foolish. How do I talk to her? How do I dance with her? Do I say anything about why she uses a chair? Too many variables outside the norm.

Oh, how I miss dancing. Luckily, both my parents have rhythm and passed those genes on to both my sister and me. Yes, I still get out on the dance floor and shake my money maker as best I can. But it is not and will never be the same. My accident happened just after Swing and Salsa dancing became popular. I would have loved to learn how to dance like that. There is something very sexy and sensual about being able to move in rhythm with the music with someone else. Dancing alone or in a group rarely causes me emotional distress. However, at times, watching couples dance together hits hard and pierces my heart because I will never stand next to my honey, hold him close and dance like that.

In all the weddings I've attended over the years, I have always gone as a single woman, both pre and post chair. Pre chair I would occasionally be asked to dance for slow songs. Post chair, I am never asked to dance. Even married or "taken" men who dance with many different women at a wedding, never approach me for a dance. Even though I am out on the floor for most fast songs, men probably would not know what the hell to do with me for a slow song. Heck, my experience was limited with dancing a slow song with a guy so even I did not know what to do. For a guy in a chair, asking a woman to dance is easier because her sitting on his lap works and looks cute. A guy would not sit on my lap, nor would I want him to. It is an awkward situation.

It is only recently that an experience changed all this. By nourishing my adventuresome spirit and giving tandem skydiving a try as a para, I befriended a crazy, fun, unconventional group of skydivers. One of the guys was getting married and my tandem instructor asked me to attend the wedding as his date. I was very excited and had a fantastic time at the wedding. I danced the fast songs as usual. When a slow song came on, one of the skydivers (not my date), took my hand, pulled me toward the dance floor and simply asked, "So, how do we do this?" Surprised, I coached him as best I could. He pulled another guy over as well and we figured out a little Jocelyn sandwich with me in the middle. For the first time since using a chair, a guy my age had asked me to dance a slow song. He did not appear freaked out or uncomfortable. He probably thought nothing of it and it was just something fun to do. He had no idea how much it meant to me. Is it a wonder that I gravitate to rather unconventional people?

While not successfully meeting anyone in person or through friends, I did give online dating a shot on and off over the course of a number of years. My greatest struggle with online dating was when to reveal that I use a chair. Using a chair is one facet of my life, but not the driving force behind it. My chair does not define me. It causes me to do activities differently, but rarely prohibits me from doing something I strongly desire to do. In the beginning, I never disclosed using a chair upfront in my posted profile or in my photos for the sake of vulnerability. With so many nutters out there, who knew what they sought. So I waited for an opportune moment, usually after a few phone conversations, but never even considered making a date and simply showing up without telling him. That would be unfair. Because men are so visual, I learned to disclose by sending photos. Simply seeing the word 'wheelchair' conjures up God only knows what sorts of images—the chair their grandma uses, an electric scooter, a chair like those borrowed at the mall. Whatever the image, it probably would be nothing like the reality of my tiny sleek chair.

Unfortunately, more often than not, after the big disclosure I never heard from the guys again. Realistically, there could be 100 different reasons why I never heard back from them, but my immediate thought is they did not want to date a woman in a chair. After it occurring at least five times, vanity took over and my ego could not take the rejection any longer. So, I decided to take a break because deep down I felt it was not the way I would meet my guy. But what do I know?

However, after some time passed, in January 2008 I decided to give online dating another try, this time for one solid year instead of a month or a few months in a row. For the first time I put in my profile that I used a chair, with photos and all. Damn it, my chair is part of me, but not all of me. One friend became very emotional as she encouraged me to put using a chair in my profile. With a shaky voice she said, "Jocelyn, you are such an amazing woman. And your having this accident and what you've done with your life despite it makes you even more amazing. You should never hide it!" I took the plunge and could not believe the sense of relief. If a guy contacted me, he knew about my chair. No more agonizing over when to tell him. Eleven years after my accident, this signified yet another step down the road of acceptance. Over the course of the year I dated a few people and even had a boyfriend for three months, but have not yet found my guy.

Thankfully, I am not the only single woman my age I know. I have plenty of single, able-bodied girlfriends who also find it hard to find the few good guys left out there. But my using a chair certainly makes it harder. Would I still be single today if I did not have a disability? Who can say?

Using a wheelchair falls significantly outside the norm of

what people encounter in the dating world. I realize men (and people in general) have questions—questions they may wonder about, but are too afraid to ask or do not know how to ask. Without asking and without knowing the real answer, people draw their own conclusions based on their assumptions. As an attractive woman paralyzed from the chest down, YES! I can have sex. I enjoy sex and do experience my own version of an orgasm although it is different from before. YES! I can get pregnant and have a natural childbirth just as any other woman. Spinal cord injuries have no impact on the reproductive system for women. And for a man accustomed to being with non-paralyzed women, sex does feel the same and not much different with a paralyzed woman.

In case you had not noticed, I am extremely independent. In a way, it may have worked against me. One of my biggest fears is men thinking they need to take care of me in more or different ways than any other able-bodied female. I also recognize that men want to be needed and feel useful. Wouldn't a guy feel manly carrying me up a flight of stairs or into an inaccessible house? I have no problem getting assistance with things I cannot do on my own. However, I have to find a balance between asserting independence and asking for and accepting assistance.

I've always been so confused about sending out the right "signals" to men. Way too often in my life I tend to be attracted to men who are—for various reasons—unavailable. After a while, with these men not showing an interest in me or not wanting to date me, I did start to wonder what the hell was wrong with me, even before my chair.

So many people would say how cool or fascinating I was. I cannot tell you how many of my friends' husbands or boyfriends tell me they absolutely love me and think I am great. I never understood how people could say these things and then a guy I am really interested in does not reciprocate the feeling. My tennis coach and good friend, Lynn, thinks I intimidate men because I am attractive, smart, successful and confident. Don't men want these qualities in a woman? Maybe they do, maybe they do not. What I do know is using a chair does not make dating easier for women.

I am a risk taker, but much less of a risk taker emotionally than physically. It is more difficult to recover from emotional scrapes than physical ones. The emotional ones tend to linger a bit longer or sometimes leave scars. The way I see it, my chair is not my only flaw. I still have all the flaws that were part of me before being in my chair. Some will say that at least my biggest one is obvious. We all have those things about ourselves that we don't want people to know right away or make a judgment based on something that may be an oddity or not our best asset—like checking to make sure the front door is locked three times every night before going to bed, snoring, ugly toe nails, butt hair, sleeping with the TV on or family scandals. So in addition to using a chair, I still have all my other imperfections. And often, people cannot get past the most obvious.

I've always been so afraid of letting people see the not-so-nice stuff that goes with being in a chair or letting people see me pissed off or in a bad mood because of it. I have bad days just like the next person and often it has absolutely nothing do to with my chair. It may be a bad hair day or I may have overslept or not slept enough. But sometimes, and it is only rare occasions, the chair itself frustrates me, makes me sad, makes me angry, makes me wish my life was not like this or makes me wonder if situations would be different if I did not use a chair. Believe it or not, I do not think *God I wish I was not in this chair* every day. Some days, sure, but most days I don't think about it at all and just carry on to do the things I need to do, in the way I need to do them, to live life.

Part of my coping mechanism is to not dwell on things. I don't spend hours contemplating *Why did this happen to me? Why can't my life be different?* Once someone asked me if I look for weekly or even daily updates on stem cell research and he seemed absolutely shocked when I said no. I said, "When something really big happens, it will be on *Dateline* and in every newspaper. Other than that, what I have today is what I have and I don't spend all my time hoping and praying to be cured." Then again, I do have use of my hands and need assistance only with a few things, such as getting things in high places or getting a boost up into a truck or SUV.

So much of my life has been spent keeping my real emotions hidden, either because I did not want others to see how I really felt or because I did not even know how I really felt. I've always been so good at achieving physical challenges—bring it on! I could recover from just about any physical injury, and being young, I never really thought anything bad would happen. That whole thing of being invincible. But when it came to emotions and allowing myself to be vulnerable to people... no thanks. That was always hard for me. And being in a chair did not change that. In fact, it perhaps made it worse because not only did I have to show people that I was completely well-adjusted to being in a chair, I did not feel like I could let go and tell people (besides my therapist) that I was depressed, sad, mad or anything besides "fine."

Like a Dementor's Kiss, needy people suck the good energy right out of me. I cannot stand to be around people who are negative, complain and only talk about themselves. It is difficult to give them much sympathy or try to help them, especially if they take no action to change their situation. They need to take matters into their own hands to make their lives better or at least show real effort in trying. I did not want people to see me as needy or as someone who bitched and moaned all the time. Sometimes I revealed my true feelings of anger or depression with my family or even a really close friend, but that was extremely rare. Why? Why could I not let this out? I did not want people to love me less. I did not want people to start to not want to talk to me or not be around me.

Using a chair drastically changes one's life in some aspects, but in other aspects it either has no bearing or sometimes is a huge magnification. Things that did not change were my personality, my stubbornness, my sense of humor, the essence of who I was (am), even if I fully did not know. I'm still trying to figure that one out. However I am making progress. My mother told me years ago (when in my early 30's) that I was very wise for someone my age. Perhaps it is just because my life experience has helped me to see things in a different perspective than some of my other peers.

Being in a chair has helped me put things in perspective. My issues of being insecure, wanting people to like me, wanting to belong in a specific group and finding the love of my life who will equally love me in return—those are the things the chair has *not* changed.

I work at a nonprofit, disability advocacy organization. The majority of my co-workers are people with disabilities, some hidden, some visible. At work we joke around and say "If you are an asshole before your disability, you'll most likely stay one after it." People can change and a disability can change someone's life, but not always in the ways people want.

In my life prior to the chair I always wanted two things:

> 1) to have people notice me when I entered a room and
> 2) to weigh 125 pounds.

I could be the poster child for the adage, "Be careful what you wish for, you just might get it." Eventually I got exactly what I wished for, but I had to have a spinal cord injury and give up physical sensation and walking to get them. People notice me alright, maybe not always when I first enter, but I do attract attention because of my chair. Not because I'm a smokin' hot chick or someone people gravitate toward.

I don't have any of the insecurities about my physical appearance, like my weight or size, anymore. Before my accident I was very dissatisfied with my appearance. Throughout my college and post college years, I thought that life would be grand if I just weighed 125 pounds. I would date more, be happier and would get more attention (the kind of attention I wanted) from men. Well, I'm thin and close to 125 pounds, but none of the things I thought would happen happened. The chair presents a whole new set of problems or if not entirely new, adds to some of the things I struggled with before the chair.

Since I've been in my chair, I look the best I've ever looked. I've been complimented more on my looks, personality and determination and people have also called me *beautiful*—I would never hear that pre-chair. But I immediately think that because one guy I want does not want me, then there is no way that all those good things about me could be true. How fucked up is that kind of thinking? And it is this thinking that is the same as before my chair. And from a logical perspective, it really makes no sense.

If some miracle cure for SCI came along, would I take advantage of it? Most likely, but this is my life now, these are my abilities now and these are my limitations now. All of it can change within a matter of seconds, not only for me, but also for you.

"Another turning point, a fork stuck in the road
Time grabs you by the wrist, directs you where to go
So make the best of this test, and don't ask why
It's not a question, but a lesson learned in time

It's something unpredictable, but in the end it's right.
I hope you had the time of your life.

—*Good Riddance (Time of Your Life)* by Green Day

Chapter Nine
Psycho in My Head

Prior to starting this book, I dug out my old journals—the ones starting in Africa and carrying forward a number of years. This put into action the advice of my godfather, Raymond, an astute intellectual who has written a number of academic books. And who, ironically, became an atheist years ago. In a conversation after my accident, I mentioned not writing as much in my journal as I did in Africa or even before my accident. With my enormous black eye from the accident, I joked about having knocked my head a bit funny somehow because of some minor behavior changes. Namely, not writing much in my journal. Also, I had pretty much stopped writing any kind of poetry. I tried a few things about Africa and friendship, but nothing like the material produced when returning from New Zealand. And most significantly, I stopped singing with the radio in the car. Ask any friend from high school about my singing with the radio. They often made fun of me because I sang with practically every song, some with real emotion. Even now I'll sometimes sing, but not like before, and not with such passion.

Raymond implored me, "Write in your journal and document all that is happening and what you feel. Never again in your life will you have this experience." So I wrote, and wrote and wrote. My journal became my confidant, my outlet, a priceless resource to examine before starting this book. I read and re-read some of the journals with utter astonishment. In all the years since my accident (at this point it had been eight years), I never once thought about reading my journals from this time period.

While I did not write every day in the months and years following my accident, the entries I did make have been monumentally helpful in taking me back to my adjustment period. They enlightened me on things long forgotten. Not being an overly emotional and expressive person when around others, reading my true thoughts and emotions offered me a different perspective than what I projected to those around me. What shocked me most was reading about how hard everything was in the beginning. How could I forget? I lived through it. It all happened to me. But I did forget. This showed me how much I had moved on and how much I accomplished.

Anyone who knew me saw the energetic, determined woman who would not let her chair stop her. I've always told people that I never went through an anger stage or had a big bout of depression where I just wanted to sit inside, eat Hostess Ho Hos, not talk to anyone and shut the world out. I simply accepted this as a major change in my life and moved on. My journals however painted a different portrait of my true thoughts. I felt much more anger and depression than I even knew. There was no big bout of depression that came and went because there was an underlying constant depression present and I did not have the self-awareness to recognize it. Plus I never let anyone see it. Only the pages of my journal drank in my rage, sadness, growth and transformation.

Projected on the exterior was a calm, deep pool of serenity, while chaos and conflict raged on the interior.

The accident was a huge life-altering experience. Who would not be depressed? But I kept the depression very hidden because I did not want people to see me as weak or vulnerable. I was not much of a crier before my accident, but cried a lot afterwards, not in front of anyone, just by myself. I became keenly aware that the more okay I was with it all, the more at ease others would be around me and less worried about how I'd fare throughout it all.

The accident definitely brought depression front and center, but the reality is that it is something I struggled with for years. I wonder if I would have had the same struggles even without my chair. Just recently I learned that in addition to my dad's depression, there was a history of it on my father's and mother's sides of my family. Since depression can be genetic, it may have been in my genes. I notice that what made me unhappy and depressed were the same issues I struggled with before I used a chair. The chair has intensified it at times, but the issues of wanting to be loved and finding my mate still overshadow even the good times in my life.

People may be shocked to hear I struggle with depression because I am motivated, almost always in a good mood and very friendly. But that is part of my wanting to put my best foot forward and not wanting people to see the chink in the armor. One time when going to one of my outpatient therapy appointments at Mary Free Bed, I cruised into the lobby area to check in and wait for my therapist. There was an able-bodied woman sitting there as well, waiting for her child to finish therapy. She asked how long I'd been in a chair and at that point it was probably about five months. She could not believe it because of the way I carried myself. She said, "I knew it just by looking at you. You're a survivor." And I guess I am.

Do survivors get depressed? Yep. And they figure out a way to adapt and prosper. To combat depression I started taking Zoloft a few years after the accident. Up until that point I forcefully resisted taking any sort of anti-depression medication. For quite a while, my psychologist urged me to take some type of antidepressant drugs. Given my dad's history with "wigging out" after he started taking Prozac, I dug my heels in when it came to taking medication. I did not want to have a similar experience or a change in my attitude or behavior as my dad had on Prozac. So I was under the illusion or delusion that taking any kind of medication would send me off the deep end. Plus, I'd see all the stuff on TV about how a little pill can make the sun shine again. I was convinced that most of the people on these drugs did not need them; they were just too lazy to work on themselves and figure out what the real problem was.

Having talked to two friends who took Zoloft for a finite period of time and said the medication helped them immensely, I decided to take the plunge and give Zoloft a trial run for at least six months. It helped immensely. A few times I tried weaning myself off the drug, but after not taking it for three months I noticed a marked difference in my moods and how I processed emotions. During those three months I dwelled more on the negative aspects of my life, cried a lot and felt enveloped in a dark cloud. Within a week of resuming my regular dose of Zoloft, I felt WAY better. I have also incorporated some holistic healing energy therapy and psychotherapy into the mix to be as mentally healthy as I can be.

A turning point in my acceptance process was my Blue Guy Day as I have come to call it. It happened two to three years after my accident. I glanced at a typical handicapped sign with the universal blue person/chair symbol. How many of those signs had I seen in my life? Since my accident? Countless. But this *one* day, the sign screamed an entirely new meaning. ME. Like the revelation of a long awaited secret, ideas and understanding rushed out of my head, down to the pen in my hand and onto the paper before me. This Blue Guy symbol was supposed to represent me? People see this Blue Guy and associate it with me? For the first time I realized my chair was one thing about myself I absolutely could not change.

We have the opportunity and option to change so much about ourselves. Being a blonde, I could change my hair color. Being 5'6" I could wear heels to be taller. I can change how I act, talk, think…but I could not change this or even do anything to hide it. You see me, you see the chair or some see the chair and then see me. There was no disguising it. While we are all prone to making snap judgments about people, I felt people made assumptions about me simply because I used a chair—assumptions about my life, my intellect, my motivation, my happiness, the kind of life I was capable of having. Based on my limited view of and exposure to disability before my accident, I knew the assumptions people made. And now I felt compelled to make an even greater effort to combat those assumptions.

While not a pretty day, it played a pivotal role in the acceptance process. Yes, my chair is something unchangeable about me. But it is not me. It is a part of who I am, it is not all of who I am. I struggled with self acceptance before my accident. So many of us struggle with it regardless of disability. Finally I started to embrace who I was as a person, including my disability.

My life has turned out nothing like I thought it would, but how it has turned out thus far is not bad. Lying in the hospital bed in Windhoek, Namibia, I never thought my life would be as good and as "normal" as it is now. I am a very logical person with faith—sometimes a little, sometimes a lot. Yet logic takes a holiday amidst the emotions of accepting loss and other life-changing events. From a logical standpoint, it makes sense that after forging ahead and moving on after a life-changing tragedy, a perceived "finish line" exists. After so many years, months, days, one thinks there *should* be a definitive point or moment where once it is passed, never again will one feel loss, grief or anger. Unfortunately, life is not like that. The grief of great loss never vanishes completely.

Grief is a funny thing. As in funny peculiar, not funny ha-ha. Grief can be a palpable force hitting you in the chest and taking your breath away. A creature all its own, it can remain dormant for years then suddenly visit at an unexpected time. Out of the blue, a smell, an action or a scene can trigger the loss and grief you thought you had put behind you.

The feeling grinds down with heaviness into your chest and hollows you out within moments. Leaving this ache. Missing something so terribly you know will never return. Do you know what a treasure it is to walk up to someone and give them a full embrace? I realize how precious it is now. Yes, people can still give me a hug, but never with the same closeness as before my chair. There is always the awkward lean of the stander with my wheels or knees in the way. But even in those moments, and thankfully that is truly what they are—moments, I do not pray for sudden physical healing, but rather for the strength to bear it. Then the rain starts, the tears flow. Grief hangs around long enough to drink its fill. Then leaves me, often a bit lighter with tear-stained cheeks.

What do I do when the dark days and moments visit? Don't they come for all of us at times? When I do have the dark days, I focus on what I have to get done. Being a single person and focusing on myself, sometimes the list is very short if not nonexistent. This can be a bad thing. In our culture we are too busy and people do not take or even make time for themselves, even if it is to sit and be quiet for 10 to 20 minutes a day. So I do keep busy, create opportunities and look outside myself and my home. The slippery slope for me is comparing my life to others' lives. And I focus on things that, to me, seem so easy for them and I imagine their lives are nearly perfect. All the while telling myself how my life does not measure up even close to theirs. I have gotten much better at stopping the landslide and that has come through practice. Being thankful for what is good has been extremely helpful. Among the bad is always some good. I keep a gratitude journal and write down five things I'm thankful for every day. Some days I stare at the page for a few moments, but I always find five things. Even if it is as basic as having a roof over my head because some people do not. My mother has often told me, "We perceive other peoples' happiness to be far greater than our own."

I drew more strength than I realized from my belief in God and my Christian roots. I learned the hard way that even though we have free will as humans, God possesses far more control in our lives than we think. God has a plan for each of us and often we remain clueless in understanding the purpose or reason for certain events. I believe some things in our lives are simply meant to happen as part of the plan. Whether in Kalamazoo on Sunday, April 13, 1997, driving a car or bounding down the steps at home or elsewhere in the world, I believe I would have acquired a spinal cord injury. This was supposed to happen in my life.

Naturally, people search for answers as to why this happened. No answers exist, or at least not answers in the concrete, cut and dry clarity we crave. As if somehow having the answer would make it all better or at least easier to live with. Even if we had the answer, we probably would not like the answer provided. Sometimes waiting for an answer's revelation proves itself worthy. But we do not live in a patient society. Over the years, I jokingly told people if I ever wrote a book I would title it *Why me?....Why Bother?* I never bothered wasting time dwelling on the why or the what if's of my accident. It happened. I can do nothing to change what happened. No one is to blame for what happened. Even if I could lay blame somewhere, what good would it do? What I can do now is make choices. Why did this happen? Who can say? I have not the slightest clue. I did not nor do I waste much time attempting to solve the 'why me?' question. What good would it do me to ask a question for which I would never obtain a satisfactory answer? I have received my strength, motivation and determination from the pure and utter grace of God. More importantly He gave me (and I accepted) the will to find those things within myself.

If I sat around all day and asked God "Why, why me? Why this?" I would never get an answer and would be tormented for the rest of my life. I'm okay without knowing a specific answer. I do take comfort and find my sanity in the belief that this is part of The Plan that God has for me. In my time spent in a chair, I think I've been a better role model to people, have been a bit more visible because of my chair and believe that I am of more use in this world in my chair than out of it.

Does that make me a bit too fatalistic? Naive? Maybe, but even if a delusion, it helps carry me through some really tough days. I imagine some of you think my view is too simplistic, that my idea of The Plan merely serves as a crutch I use to hobble around the landmines set off throughout the course of life. As I paraphrase from C.S. Lewis in *Mere Christianity*, "So what?" Believing somehow good will come out of this horrible accident, that somehow I will be of more use to this world in my wheelchair than out of it, has given me hope and light at some of my darkest moments.

It all came down to the choices I made and looking back it

is purely by God's grace and how He made me that I was able to make the choices I did. I could not imagine having done anything differently because it is not my character. I see how hard it really was in the beginning and how much I really hated being in a chair. But I was not bitter or pissed at the world. Perhaps it is a product of being in my family—even if there is something wrong, don't talk about it, just pretend everything is fine.

Reading my feelings and my thoughts from my journals since the accident until now makes me realize how far I truly have come. A sense of freedom and elation comes from such realizations and reaching milestones like the Blue Guy Day. Looking back, I can see such milestones more easily. Another such feat was the day I threw away my orthotics—shoe inserts used to correct how one walks. When I began running cross country my freshman year in high school, through an injury I discovered my feet pronated significantly. Pronation is the foot leaning and rolling inward. To correct the problem, I went to a podiatrist for a custom made pair of orthotics. Which I discovered I had to wear not only when running, but all the time. Even after my accident, I kept them. I do not really know why. They were tossed in a box with a plethora of other things which had no real place, yet were things I did not want to throw out. Every time I moved, they came with me. Six years after my accident, getting ready to move again, I sorted through the box to see if I could get rid of anything. I picked up my orthotics. I turned them over in my hands, ran my fingers over the edges and the dip of the heel. I brought my bare left foot up onto my lap and pressed the orthotic in its place, seeing, but not feeling, the perfect mold to my heel and arch. Releasing my foot back onto my foot plate with watery eyes, I turned and tossed them in the trash. The time felt right to let them go. I had no need for them or to hang onto them.

"He will either protect you from suffering or give you unfailing strength to bear it..."

—St. Francis de Sales

Chapter Ten
Grace

When I left my comfortable, sheltered home for college, I felt free! Liberated from scrutiny and watchful eyes asking me where I was going, who I would be with, when would I be home and, without fail, the Friday question, "When are you going to go to church this weekend?" As a cradle Catholic, born and raised in the tradition, I absorbed my parents' view of faith. Go to mass once a week, say grace at meals, say your prayers at night, work hard, be good and all will be right in the universe. Church did not factor into the equation of my new found freedom. I relished making my own decisions, knowing my parents had no control over what I did or did not do in Ann Arbor.

Between the ages of thirteen to sixteen, teenagers in the Catholic faith make the sacrament of Confirmation. During this sacrament, the teenager professes to their belief and dedication to the Catholic church. How can a teenager at that age truly know what he/she believes? Their beliefs at that age most likely reflect the beliefs of their parents. Confirmation, while a holy and meaningful sacrament, is something many teenagers do out of obligation rather than true belief. If the church waited until children reached the ages of eighteen or twenty, I speculate a very low percentage of people would seek out Confirmation on their own. At some point, children commonly rebel against their parents' beliefs. I do not know about you, but my beliefs differed greatly at the age of twenty than at thirteen. Likewise, my beliefs in my thirties are different from when I was twenty. There comes a time in adulthood when we children claim our faith and our beliefs as our own, whatever that may be and however different it may be from how we were raised.

My accident launched me on my own faith journey, bringing me back to my roots and allowing me to claim my own faith, although I did not recognize it at the time. Nor did I think while in the Namibian hospital, "God is taking care of me." However, looking back on the entire experience through my faith-colored glasses, I see how He helped me, watched over me and, in a way, "spoke" to me. I can honestly say I have never heard "the voice of God." Some lucky people I know unequivocally say, "I heard His voice and God said to me..." or perhaps they experienced a feeling so strong it felt like God's voice. My dialogues with God tend to be rather one-sided—my side. I talk to Him a lot, but never hear much back. I wish I heard His voice. I wish He would be direct and vocal with me so I can find out what the hell He wants me to do with my life.

I always believed in God. When in college I may have leaned toward Agnosticism, while always knowing a Higher Power existed. The whole idea of the Son dying on the cross for the world's sins did not hold much water for me during those years. Even though I was raised in the Catholic faith and attended Catholic school for thirteen years, it was never the culture of "Jesus is the only way to salvation." I was raised believing good people go to heaven, regardless of their faith. I am so thankful to have been raised with that belief system. It stuck with me.

When my parents separated and my mother's world fell apart, she turned to her faith for support. She entered into a seven-year, nondenominational Bible study that revitalized her faith. She began the classes during my New Zealand trip, so she already had a few years under her belt when my accident occurred. To keep my spirits up when she thought I needed a pick-me-up, she gave me note cards with Bible verses on them. Coming from a family that never read the Bible together and only prayed together during church and at meals, this was a drastic change from the mother I had known as a child. When in the hospital in Windhoek, she read stories to me from the Bible. Rehabilitation back in the States kept me busy. My down time filled up with rest, visitors and phone calls with no time for pleasure reading, let alone the Bible.

While I credit my mother for being a crucial stepping stone on my spiritual journey, hindsight reveals many significant stepping stones even at the sand dune immediately after my accident. People often ask me, "How did you stay so calm? How did you adjust so well?" From the first moment I realized I was paralyzed, I possessed an unexplainable serenity. My cop out response is usually along the lines of, "I don't know. This is how God made me and how I'm wired. I could not imagine reacting any other way because it is not my nature." Looking back on the course of events, the people in my life, my reaction and coping skills, I see the sheer grace of God as the "how." He was with me through all of it, even though I did not recognize it at the time.

My serenity in calmly accepting my circumstances, from lying paralyzed at the bottom of the dune to Dr. Schroeder saying, "I want you to know you'll probably never walk again," not only sounds implausible to others, it also surprises me. If someone were to have asked me, "What would you do if you were ever in the middle of a desert, paralyzed and not able to walk again?" flashes of myself weeping inconsolably or hanging onto life by wispy gossamer may have crossed my mind. Whatever I would have answered, it would not have mirrored my actual behavior. Even at the hospital in Windhoek, my mother attributed my tranquility to the presence of the Holy Spirit. At the time, I thought, *OK, Mom, whatever,* like an exasperated teenager. I am now much farther along my spiritual path and share her belief.

The path of acceptance is long, sometimes treacherous, sometimes enlightening. At times I felt God right there with me, at other times it felt like He took a holiday and forgot all about me. Like a burst of bright light in an A-ha! moment, so has it been for some moments of clarity on my spiritual journey. Within a year or two of the accident, the story of the conversion of St. Paul the Apostle popped into my head one afternoon while writing in my journal.

Chapter nine in *Acts of the Apostles* tells Saul's story. He took the name Paul after his conversion. Saul was a Pharisee and a free Roman citizen who ruthlessly persecuted early Christians because he believed they were heretics against the Jewish faith. While he was riding on the road to Damascus to arrest Christian men and women, a bright blinding light flashed in front of him. He fell from his horse, heard the voice of Jesus ask why Saul persecuted Him and His disciples, and was left unable to see. Following Jesus' instructions, Saul's companions led Saul into Damascus where he spent three days without sight. Finally, a disciple named Ananias came to Saul, "Placing his hands on Saul, he said, 'Brother Saul, the Lord—Jesus, who appeared to you on the road as you were coming here—has sent me so that you may see again and be filled with the Holy Spirit.' Immediately, something like scales fell from Saul's eyes and he could see again." (Acts 9: 17-18).

I compared my own accident to this conversion story. Saul had the shock of blinding light and falling from his horse. I had the shock of flying off my board and instant paralysis. He had companions to lead him into Damascus, I had companions to watch over and be with me. He spent three days in Damascus without sight, I spent about three hours without sight; he had a scale-like substance over his eyes, I had encrusted sand over mine. God sent Ananias to remove the scales so Saul could finally see. Craig, the paramedic, removed the sand from my eyes and restored my vision. Hindsight revealed to me that my accident and everything happening prior to reaching the hospital was the marked beginning of finding faith and God for myself.

A large part of my inner healing and acceptance included lots of journal writing. One afternoon while writing, I thought about flying home on the stretcher. Naturally my mind raced to Peter and Ruth. Suddenly, it occurred to me that those were two Biblical figures, each with their own book in the Bible; Peter actually has two books. I wondered if this could be another way God was speaking to me, but until then I had not listened. I immediately searched for my Bible, wondering if these books contained any messages or spiritual nuggets to digest.

Opening to the first page of the introduction to *Ruth,* words leapt out at me from the side of the page Key Message: "God does not leave us in hard times." The bold face key theme in the sidebar was Redemption. Seeing the applicability to my life, I excitedly flipped the pages to find *Peter I.* Likewise, I found on the introduction page another Key Message: "Stand fast in the true grace of God." The key theme was Hope for the hurting. Unbeknownst to me at the time, God provided signals to me that He was with me the entire time. At that point in my life, I cannot say I was "with Him." He was more like the friend you ring up when you really need something and you know he/she will help you out in a bind. Even possessing the wisdom to make such a connection and look for a message from those who protectively escorted me back home is a gift from God.

When I said goodbye to Ruth and Peter at Detroit Metro airport, Ruth wrote down her address for me. A few years after my accident, I did write to her to give her an update. I never received a response, nor was the letter returned to me. Two people simply doing their everyday jobs, yet they have no idea of the true impact they had on my life. It is the nature of their work to bid farewell to the many people they have escorted home from all over the world over the years and never hear from any of them again.

Although it's a cliché, the Lord truly works in mysterious ways. Firsthand experience and a heightened post-accident awareness helped me identify some of those elusive methods. Nurturing and growing in faith is not synonymous with attending church. Growing up and attending mass on Sunday provided me with a structure around which to build my faith.

For a year after my accident, I prayed, read the Bible a bit, but did not attend church. For Lent in 1998, I decided to *do* something rather than give something up, as is the common practice. I designated finding a church and attending Mass each Sunday of Lent as my "to do." Living on the northwest side of Grand Rapids, I chose The Parish of the Holy Spirit, a Catholic Church. It looked new and extremely accessible. I felt a little intimidated going by myself, but I made a commitment and I stuck by it. My Lenten commitment that year carried on past Easter and to this day I attend church frequently.

I remained a member of Holy Spirit for a few years. I joined a Bible study group and became more involved in the parish than we ever had done as a family. We attended church each week, my parents put their envelope in the basket, but they rarely served on committees or participated in any church activities. When I began working full time on the southeast side of Grand Rapids, I moved to the southeast side of town from my apartment on the northwest side. I adored my priest at Holy Spirit and for a few weeks made the nearly 30-minute drive to church, but it started to wear on me. My boss suggested I check out St. Stephens, where a good friend of his, Father Mark, was the pastor. I decided to try it since it was only a 15-minute drive. I instantly loved Father. Mark and the parish. Friendly people and a priest who gave a wonderful connect-the-scriptures-to-daily-life homily each week scored big points in my book. I had found a new parish.

As a way to meet people in the parish, I signed up for another Bible Study class. My experience with Bible Studies at Holy Spirit had been a group of mainly older, married women—not young, single people my age, let alone, single men my age. But I signed up for Bible Study to learn about the Bible, not meet a husband. Plus, *Ruth* and *Esther* were the two books selected for study. *Ruth?* How could I pass?

While beautiful and richly characteristic due to its age, St. Stephens was old and not ideally accessible...but manageable. Holy Spirit had a greater degree of accessibility because it had been rebuilt in the early 1990's. To register for Bible Study, I emailed the Religious Ed office at St. Stephens and inquired where the class would be held and its degree of accessibility. St. Stephens had a school attached to the church and a fairly new wing had been added to the school. Luckily, the class would be held in new part, with a fully functioning elevator. The woman in the office provided me with excellent directions for parking and entering the building.

On a Wednesday evening early in September 2000, I worked late, then headed to St. Stephens for the Bible Study class starting at 7:00 P.M. I saw a few cars in the parking lot as I pulled in. As I went through my getting out of the car routine, a few people trickled out of the building. It looked as if something had just wrapped up before the Bible Study began. I easily entered the building, found the elevator and took it down to the basement. The doors opened into a room that appeared to be the teacher's lounge. I meandered through the lounge, empty at this hour, and found the door to the hallway. Whew! Totally accessible. What a breeze! I wandered down the brightly lit hallway, looking into the window of each classroom as I passed by, but found no one around. It was 6:55 P.M. I thought it a bit odd that all the rooms were empty. Indeed, something had been wrapping up as I arrived, but it did not look as if something else would be starting. This was only the first or second week in September. Having left the email printout of the directions for the class at the office, I concluded I got the week wrong. The class probably started the following week.

I shrugged my shoulders, turned around to head back upstairs, satisfied I knew where to go next week and the level of accessibility of the place. Making my way back to the elevator, I approached the door to the teacher's lounge which had closed behind me as I entered the hall. Reaching for the lever door handle, I grasped it, pushed down to swing the door open, but the handle did not move. It was locked. "Oh, Shit!" rushed out of my mouth, forgetting I was in a Catholic school. Looking down the empty hallway and seeing the doors to the stairwells wide open, I contemplated my options, which were few. Once again, the McGuyver in me stepped up to the plate. I took out my Swiss Army knife and attempted to pick the lock on the door. Let's just say it is a good thing I did not opt for a life of crime. The attempt lasted all of an entire minute.

Without access to the elevator, I literally was trapped. Thank God for cell phones! I called the operator to get the number of the police dept. This by no means constituted an emergency situation, thus I did not call 911. Once connected to the East Grand Rapids Police Dept, waiting for someone to answer, I sat there laughing. I felt so ridiculous. Someone answered the phone and I explained my predicament, "Oh, hi…um…I'm trapped in the basement of St. Stephens' church. I use a wheelchair and the door to get back to the elevator is locked." You know they did not get calls like this every day. The woman told me someone would come to get me. I let out a sigh of relief. Had I not gotten any cell reception in the basement, option number 3 was to pull the fire alarm, which, while illegal, was the only thing I could think of to bring people to the building before 7 A.M. the next morning.

Ten minutes later, at the far end of the hallway, the door opened and a police officer came down the hall accompanied by a guy in his twenties who introduced himself as Matt. Another Matt in my life to be with me in times of great need. Matt asked, "Are you looking for the Bible Study group?" I replied, "Yes!! I was told to come here for it." Matt said they were meeting on the other side of the building, the older side. I thanked both of them for coming to my rescue. Matt had the keys to open the teacher lounge door. He escorted me up in the elevator and to the other side of the building which also had an elevator, but one of those really small, closet type elevators. Though an old church, St. Stephens did what it could to be as accessible as it could be given its structure.

I felt like an idiot and wondered how the woman in the Religious Ed office got the location so wrong. Matt good naturedly helped me get downstairs and brought me into the Youth Ministry room. The group was in the middle of saying a Rosary. I quietly found a spot in the circle, parked myself and observed the group members. The room contained about 10 to 15 people, all in their twenties and thirties. I felt like I just joined my high school youth group. As the Rosary ended, the discussion topic for the evening got underway and it was not *Ruth* and *Esther*. I thought, *oh, my God. This is the wrong group*. In that moment, grace helped me realize I had stumbled upon the perfect group for me.

Another significant stepping stone on my spiritual path. That is how I discovered my young adult Bible study group, which I faithfully attended for the next five years. In reading over the email print out directions at work the next day, I learned I did indeed have the wrong day. The *Ruth* and *Esther* Bible Study began the following week. Talk about the Lord working in mysterious ways. Had I never gotten trapped in the basement, I never would have found the perfect group for me. If the door to the teacher lounge had been open, I would have simply gotten in my car, driven home, and returned the following week knowing nothing of the young adult group meeting a few hundred feet from me.

In the early years of attending the group, I went to confession during a weekend retreat. This was the first time I'd been to confession since high school. The opportunity was presented to me, so I accepted it. I told the priest about my accident and gave him a synopsis of my spiritual life. He had an interesting take on the situation. He said to me, "How blessed are you?"

"What?" I replied with a look somewhere between perplexed and are-you-freaking-kidding-me. Among all the words to describe my accident, paralysis and using a wheelchair, blessing did not make the list. Well, I would not consider being paralyzed and in a wheelchair a "blessing."

With a nod of peaceful reassurance he explained, "God used your accident to call you back to Him." This time I listened and started my own spiritual journey.

It's funny how my perspective on life has changed. My thought process for decision making, at times, can be very different from before the accident. If a task or occasion arises which I'm not excited about, but know I should do, my line of reasoning is usually, "I waited at the bottom of a sand dune, paralyzed with a broken back in Namibia for three and a half hours, I'm sure I can endure…(fill in the blank with just about anything). One such instance was attending my dad's wedding. I would not go to the ceremony, but could endure stopping by the reception for a half hour. Thank God my friend Mary came with me.

Also, in terms of accepting the big change in my life, I think I did pretty well with moving on. In talking to other paras or quads that I've met since being injured, I'm thankful my injury resulted from a decision that I had made—to go (down the dune) or not to go? That was the question. No one else caused my paralysis by shooting me with a gun or running into me with a car. I had no one to blame but me. And while I *could* have spent time, energy and emotion beating myself up over my decision, I never did.

"Don't ask yourself what the world needs. Ask yourself what makes you come alive, and go do that, because what the world needs is people who have come alive."

-Gil Bailie

Chapter Eleven
I Am the Tortoise

When working at Applebee's as a bartender between my New Zealand and Africa trips, I grew to know some of the regulars quite well, some of whom I began to hang out with outside the restaurant. One such regular was Mark, a guy about my age, with short light brown hair, a slim build, and who spoke with a very slight lisp. He typically came in alone, and as he visited more often, he became friendly with some of the employees.

One night a fellow tender and I went to Mark's to play games. We decided to play Balderdash,—a game in which players make up word definitions and people have to pick out the real definition. I had heard of Balderdash, but never played. I figured being an English major would come in handy. I got off to a painfully slow start. Everyone else leapt far ahead of me. Obviously I had overestimated my skill and knowledge when it came to this game. Then, suddenly, after a few good turns, I caught up to the pack. After a few more good turns, I ended up winning the game!

As I drove home thinking about the evening, I realized the game, and what just played out, could be a metaphor for my life. Instantly the story of *The Tortoise and the Hare* popped into my head and I blurted out, "I'm the fucking tortoise!" The Tortoise appeared to be far behind in the foot race with the Hare, with no hope of catching up. After a quick start and establishing an enormous lead, the Hare eventually exhausted himself, which allowed the Tortoise to catch up, pass him and win the race.

I always compared (and sometimes still do) my life to my friends' lives, looking at what they possessed or accomplished. I do not recommend this as a means of achieving good mental health and high self esteem. Such comparison rarely results in a realization of all the good things we have; rather, it spotlights what we consider the holes or inadequacies in our lives. Moreover, we come to believe everyone judges us by those standards. I always felt inadequate compared to everything my friends had possessed or achieved at particular stages their lives. While other friends went on to obtain professional degrees and start careers, I waited tables and traveled around the world. Driving home from Mark's, like someone turning on the light in a dark closet, an "A-ha"! moment struck. Suddenly I understood I do not move at the same pace as everyone else, but catch up or come out ahead in the end.

During Christmas of 2005, my two-year-old nephew received the Sesame Street Chutes and Ladders game as a gift. He started playing with Gretchen, my five-year-old nephew, and me, but lost interest. At the beginning of the game I landed on a ladder and moved way ahead of everyone, then got sent down a long chute which left me far behind. As the game progressed, my nephew was one spot away from winning and just needed to spin a one to win. Before he took his turn, I landed on the ladder shooting me straight to the top to win the game. I do not tell you this to gloat over beating my young nephew, but rather to point out the Tortoise theme cropping up, once again, years after the evening at Mark's. At a time when I had been feeling bad about not being married and not having kids. I was not even dating anyone. But in a simple game of Chutes and Ladders, God reminded me my life will all work out in the end. I know I don't go at the same pace as others, but knowing it and coming to be at peace with it in my heart are two very different things.

In life, we are sent the same lessons to learn over and over again until we learn them. Despite that moment of clarity for my natural tortoise-like pattern, I still think somehow in life I will simply be like everyone else. I do not know what part of me thinks that somehow this vital, innate core of my soul and being is going to change. Obviously, some part of me does, and it is that part that has not yet learned this lesson. I frequently underestimate the value of traveling around the world, whether with a group or alone. As I wandered around the world seeking different adventures, I felt envious of my friends who had a plan, had goals to achieve and knew what professions they wanted to pursue. And they, in turn, were envious of me traveling around the world while they worked to pursue their goals. Without even knowing it, deep down, I bucked the typical American standards for success.

As an icebreaker at a recent strategic planning session for work, the consultant we worked with had each of us write on a piece of paper what we wanted to be when we grew up. Of the ten people in the room, some quickly wrote down their answer and gave it to our consultant. I stared at my blank sheet of paper for minutes. I did not know what to put down. As a child or high school student, what had I wanted to be? The consultant got ready to complete the icebreaker exercise, but I stopped him because my sheet remained blank. I had to put down something and everyone waited for me. I quickly scribbled Astronaut and gave my paper to him. Yes, at one time I did want to be an astronaut. However, that dream quickly died when I discovered the amount of math and science required for such a career. I'm not opposed to working hard, but math and science…no thanks.

I never knew what I wanted to be when I grew up. I still don't. In college and afterwards, choosing one career path or one thing to do seemed impossible. Part of my indecision stemmed from too many career choices. I literally could be anything I wanted to be. That sort of monumental decision at a young age paralyzed me with fear. Yes, me. Being so overwhelmed it seemed easier to do nothing than to select a career. But in reality, my "fear" did not paralyze me at all, it set me in motion, on many paths around the world, eventually leading me to a paralysis I could not escape and could in no way conceal. It forced me to decide upon some means of livelihood to support myself and start a career.

My job at the bookstore fit my lifestyle and needs at the time. People would often say to me, "It must be so great to work here." Yes, it was a stimulating, good-vibe environment. However, much like the restaurant industry, it was still customer service which brings encounters with all sorts of interesting folks. At times I've been tempted to write a book about my work experiences in the restaurant industry and at the bookstore. The title I had in mind? *At The Registers* because all the interesting stories usually took place while cashing people out.

One evening, two or three of us were working at the

registers. The register desk was a semicircle and my register was off to the right of the main register. With about five people in line, I glanced up and made eye contact with a woman about four people back. In a jovial manner, she kind of yelled over to me—past all the others ahead of her—"Hey, no sitting down on the job!" I just laughed, because from where she stood, she could not see I used a wheelchair. As she approached to cash out and saw I used a wheelchair, the jovial look quickly fell and transformed into mortification. Her mouth hung open for a moment before she started apologizing profusely about her comment. I took it in good stride and took no offense since she was clearly embarrassed and meant no disrespect.

The flip side of those situations are ones that cause me to wonder *what the hell are people thinking?* One evening, while cashing out a man in his mid-forties buying one or two books, we made idle chit chat. Toward the end of the transaction, he casually asked me, "So, have you been crippled your whole life?" I stopped instantly and thought *he did not say what I think he said.* I looked at him and said in disbelief, "WHAT?" He repeated the question and oh, yes, he said what I thought he said. If he had been an 80-year-old person, I would not have been as offended. "Crippled" is a word he would have grown up with as part of his culture, like my grandparents. But a 40-year-old guy? Come on! Being so stunned I simply replied, "No, I had an accident."

He quickly retorted, "Oh, so you were doing something you were not supposed to be doing." Again, with a stunned, incredulous look on my face, I said, "No." Rather smugly he informed me, "Well, lucky for me, I was saved before

I died." Meaning that before he left this earthly world he accepted Jesus Christ as his Savior. Implying I must not be a good Christian person, and God was clearly punishing me for being a bad person. But praise the Lord, nothing like a spinal cord injury could happen to him, because he is "saved." So many people have asked, "Did you ask him if he's been an idiot all his life? No, I did not. Being so new to using a chair, I was too surprised to respond quickly with some biting remark. If something similar happened today, I would be much more inclined to unabashedly express my opinion about the wording of the question and the level of his intelligence.

While working at the bookstore and continuing to adjust to life using a chair, I made no effort to become part of any spinal cord injury support group or connect with any disability groups in town. My current boss at Disability Advocates, Dave, has since told me that many times he would come into the bookstore, see me and be tempted to approach me, give me his business card and say, "You need to be a part of us." If he had, I would have smiled politely, nodded my head and filed his card right in the trash after he left. Not that I had a bad attitude about having a disability, but I considered myself to be upbeat and motivated. One of my misconceptions about people with disabilities at the time included their being a bunch of pissers and moaners. Why would I want to surround myself with bad energy when I just wanted to move ahead in my life? I also received invites to the Mary Free Bed spinal cord support group, but never felt compelled to attend.

Little did I know, accessibility advocacy and a career with

Disability Advocates awaited me just around the bend. My first taste of advocacy (or rather social injustice) took place in 1998 when the movie theaters in Grand Rapids began converting to stadium seating. A friend from Schuler's and I went to one cinema that already converted two of their theaters. Much to my dismay, the theater placed all accessible seating in the front row. Very few people choose to sit in the front row. I found myself in an awkward situation. I had not known my friend for very long and I wondered if I should say anything about not being able to sit that close to the screen. Aside from getting a sore neck, so much motion up close would make me sick. I did not want him to think I was a wimp or a pain in the ass. So, I decided to see how it went. The movie started and 10 minutes later we found ourselves at the ticket counter asking for our money back. Neither of us could take sitting that close to the screen. They refunded our money and my friend was totally cool with it.

The more I thought about it, the more alarmed I became—*theaters can't all be like that!* I love going to movies. With the old ramp style seating, I could choose seating near or far from the screen and jump into a seat while a friend whisked my chair to the back of the theater. With stadium seating, the theater design dictated where my friends and I sat. Steps going up to all the seats really limited where and at what distance from the screen I could sit. People grow accustomed to the freedom of making all of their own choices. I pay the same price for a movie ticket as everyone else; given the availability of seats, should I also not be able to choose where I sit in the theater as everyone else does? I kept thinking, *This is wrong. How can they do this? Now I have no choice only because I sit and use wheels instead of walk?*

When expressing my outrage to one of my therapists at Mary Free Bed, she suggested I contact Disability Advocates of Kent County. Putting aside all my misconceived notions about people with disabilities and disability-related organizations, I called. Why? Because now I personally felt discriminated against. My cheek still prickled with the sting of injustice. I wanted action taken to prevent all the theaters in Grand Rapids from restricting the accessible seating to only the front row. When I called Disability Advocates, I spoke to Megan, head of the Access Team. She invited me to their office to meet with her and Dave, the disability rights organizer. Upon meeting Megan, it surprised me to learn she also used a wheelchair due to a spinal cord injury. I instantly liked her—not just because of the chair. With a personality to match her bright clothes and big hair, she greeted me warmly. She too felt excited about having another woman in a chair involved in advocacy.

Dave was soon introduced to the woman he always wanted to recruit from the bookstore but never did. Hmmm, rather ironic. As Megan and Dave listened intently, I explained in more detail my experience at the movie theater. Being green to advocacy, I left it to the experts to assemble a plan of action.

The following week, we scheduled meetings with the two main theaters in town that started their renovations. Megan and Dave went with me to both meetings. Between the two theaters, one was much more receptive to meeting with us than the other. In fact, when we went to the more receptive theater for a meeting, the manager said that they had actually started renovation on their theaters and stopped after attending a conference that laid out a much better design for accessible seating. The other theater had plans for all of its theaters to have more accessible seating options than just the front row, but the staff was not as welcoming to us.

My first attempt at advocacy had worked out well. With the positive outcome of meeting with the theater staff and a sense of appreciation for Disability Advocates' assistance, I began volunteering at Disability Advocates one day a week. Without a clear direction, I continued inching along my path. Flinging myself with wild abandon into the arms of disability rights advocacy did not suit me. I needed time to get my feet wet. Yes, people say it's better to dive right in so your body absorbs the shock all at once, rather than creeping in at a snail's pace. But I followed my instinct, and eventually took the plunge.

One of the first tasks assigned to me as a volunteer was assisting with an accessibility review of a local college. I had no previous experience doing reviews or prior knowledge of construction standards for accessibility, but I did have enthusiasm and a desire to learn. Disability Advocates taught me what I needed to know and I worked in conjunction with a staff person, not only learning more about building codes for wheelchair access, but more about signage, handrails and step configuration to accommodate other disabilities. Broadening my perspective, I now had a greater understanding of the disability world. My misconceptions about persons with disabilities—they are lazy, uneducated, complainers and poor—evaporated. Heck, think of those you know who possess those characteristics and have *no* disability.

After a year of volunteering at Disability Advocates (all the while working at the bookstore), I took the leap and applied for a fulltime job with Disability Advocates, to assist with their fundraising and community education. Although not the heavens-opening, lightening-bolt revelation I would have preferred to reinforce certainty, I began sensing a purpose for my accident. If I, as a person with a disability, possessed all kinds of misconceptions and negative impressions about people with disabilities—then the majority of the world most likely shared those misconceptions too. The injustice! When offered the opportunity to have a hand in educating and dispelling these negative misconceptions, I jumped at the chance. Reminiscent of the bookstore, I was offered the first fulltime job I applied for as a person using a chair.

I must confess, what people perceive as die-hard advocacy from me, is sometimes pure selfishness. Sorry to be a bubble buster. With the movie theater advocacy, I simply did not want to sit in the front row. Was I the only one? No. The theater conversion must have incensed others, but they were not my motivation for exploring what could be done to prevent only front row accessible seating. When I first started working fulltime at Disability Advocates, they offered health insurance, but no dental. I asked if I could look into the cost of dental insurance and was given the Okay to do so. After some investigation, dental insurance proved to be a reasonable expense Disability Advocates could share with its employees. After providing a cost analysis, the Board approved it. Some employees later came to thank me for doing the investigating and presentation, but again—it was all about me. I wanted dental insurance. Maybe it is a character trait of being the baby in the family—wanting to get my own way. Now that I am older and mature, oh, I still like getting my way; however, if it does not happen, I don't whine or cry about it anymore like I did at the age of five.

In relation to advocacy, I do not make unreasonable demands expecting changes to happen. But I do expect to be treated as everyone else and not as a second class citizen simply because I use wheels for mobility instead of legs. I tend to speak up about things because it is simply the right thing to do. I had the good fortune of completing my college education before my accident and was blessed with good people skills and the ability to speak articulately. Now, in retrospect, I feel a responsibility to speak for those who cannot, and to show the able-bodied population the kind of life that is possible despite having a disability.

When waking every morning to start my day, I do not think *What injustice can I take on today?* I just live my life. Example is a huge part of leadership, or good leadership, anyway. I'm a firm believer in "people will not go where they are not led." I don't think there is any child out there whose parents have not said, "Do as I say, not as I do." That was a familiar phrase around my house growing up. Children might accept such a saying from an authority figure, but with adults it does not go over so well.

Looking at my life, the pattern seems to be that what happens is usually the result of my reacting to something rather than my making a plan to achieve a goal by following steps. I'm much more of a fly-by-the-seat-of-my-pants kind of woman. And somehow it all works out. Most likely a great deal of Divine intervention occurs unbeknownst to me. Working part-time after my accident, writing in my journals, both long before and long after the accident and choosing not to pack my life with busyness from dawn til dusk has given me time to reflect on everything that has brought me to the here and now. I am becoming much more aware of Divine intervention in my life—the people who come into my life, the sequence of events as they occur, not getting what I wanted, getting something else that was so much better for me—and, appreciating, most of the time, that Someone is looking out for me.

As far as a career or accomplishing things in my life, I've never looked at my chair as any kind of barrier, within reason. Am I going to climb Mt. Everest? No, but I did not want to before my chair either. As far as career paths, I do not see my chair hindering me at all. I can do whatever I want. Narrowing it down has always been the struggle. My accident certainly was good for grounding me to stay in one place for an extended period of time. Heck, my "plan" after returning from Ireland was to explore working for a company in California that did bike and kayak trips to various places around the globe. Obviously that did not happen.

"I went to the woods because I wished to live deliberately, to front only the essential facts of life, and see if I could not learn what it had to teach, and not, when I came to die, discover that I had not lived. I did not wish to live what was not life, living is so dear...I wanted to live deep and suck out all the marrow of life..."

—From *Walden* by Henry David Thoreau

CHAPTER TWELVE
STILL A THRILL SEEKER

Using a chair is an adventure. Not usually in a fun, blow-your-hair-back kind of way, but rather in a you-never-know-what-will-happen kind of way. You need to be ready for the unexpected—both the good and not so good. The good being someone holding the door open for you or fetching something from the high shelf in the grocery store. The not so good being a flat tire, a wheel rolling away while getting out of the car or my bladder not cooperating as I would like. The fun never stops. It's a good thing I enjoy a bit of excitement in life.

I have always loved taking on physical challenges. The thought of getting seriously injured or hurt never crossed my mind. The bungee jumping, tandem skydiving, white water rafting, I loved it all. How could anything happen? We wore safety gear. Older folks think kids are a bunch of dumb asses for doing such daring feats. The kids love the rush, the fun, and feeling invincible. But after a serious or disabling accident or injury, the feeling of invincibility melts away. Like a force field deactivating, vulnerability unsettles people who think they can accomplish anything. Often, after a temporary hiatus, the thrill seeker in them typically returns. Some people do not skip a beat, and scare the hell out of the nurses and therapists during rehab with popping wheelies or racing around in their chairs. I kept my penchant for thrill seeking, with perhaps just a bit more caution.

During rehab, I was not one of the rabble rousers testing

the limits of the nurses and the wheelchair equipment. I really should learn to bounce down a curb while popping a wheelie and go down steep ramps while in a wheelie, but have not yet mastered those skills. Mainly because I do not practice, and usually people are around to help or a curb cut may be near, though not right in front of me. Because my paralysis begins at my bra line, I have no abdominal support and horrible balance. Not only do I fear flipping over backwards and splitting my head open or breaking my neck, but also losing my balance and falling out frontwards if I tried these things. While this is an area in which I display some caution, in other areas, like snow skiing, water skiing, traveling, I do not hold back. These are things that thrilled me before I lived my life in a chair and I still do them today.

When in rehab, Mindy, my recreational therapist, introduced me to wheelchair sports. First she asked what sorts of activities I enjoyed. While I led an active lifestyle, I did not participate in any organized sports, like an adult softball or volleyball team. My sister was the softball and basketball player. In little league softball I sat in right field on my mitt, picking at the grass while she played a more exciting position. My activity consisted of walking and biking. Occasionally running, but only when I needed to really burn off steam. In high school I did run track—the 800m (half mile) was my event—but as I got older, I realized I hated running. Even though I wore my headphones and listened to music, I focused too much on how every step hurt. I would rather have walked six miles than run it even though it would take longer. I know, it sounds strange especially since I now get the urge to run when spring rolls around, maybe because track season was in the spring.

However, having the urge would not necessarily turn me into a runner again.

Since I had an inclination to try new, exciting and adventurous things, Mindy gave me information on various recreational activities. However, sports and hobbies did not rank high on my priority list. I remained focused on learning to live in and use a chair. While therapists want to show what is possible, as was the case when Dr. Schroeder called my room that evening and wanted me to turn on the televised wheelchair basketball game, the newly injured person has to want to participate in such activities. I knew I would try some wheelchair sports at some point, but not *right* after my accident.

Luckily, I kept in touch with Mindy after my release from Mary Free Bed and was still in outpatient therapy as the summer of '97 approached. With encouragement (and help with a ride) from Mindy, we went to watch a water ski clinic sponsored by Mary Free Bed in July. I was very curious as to how it was all going to work. Even quads could water ski. Once I arrived and watched others, I wanted to try it so badly. It looked exhilarating, exciting and fun. Imagine a single wide water ski, about as wide as a kneeboard (a 20-inch-wide board on which one kneels while being pulled by a boat) and a bit longer than a regular water ski that is slotted at the tip so the tow rope can be knotted and placed in the slot to pull the ski. Then, a seating contraption called a cage is mounted onto the ski and the skier sits in it. The size of the cage varies depending on the size of the skier. One size does not fit all. The cage needs to fit the skier snuggly, but not so tightly that the person has a hard time getting out. The skier is not strapped in because when the person falls over, she needs to be able to get out of the cage and swim up to the surface.

When starting out, as with stand up water skiing, the ski is in the water with the person sitting in the cage. For a beginner's ski, the tow rope is placed in the slot at the top of the ski. To get going, an able-bodied person hangs onto the back of the cage as the boat starts to pull the ski. This lifts the tip of the ski out of the water and stabilizes the ski until it is up and running. Once the skier is cruising, the person drops off. With dropping the extra weight of a person, the boat lunges forward. For quads, an additional back support is added to the cage so that the person can lean against it. For others, who have enough stability and hand function, they lean forward over their knees and release the tow rope from the slot. Suddenly, they're water skiing!! For more advanced skiers there is an intermediate ski which is narrower than the beginner's and then an advanced ski which is narrower yet. The slimmer the ski the better the carving and turning responsiveness. Intermediate and advanced skis do not have slots at the top; by that time, the person starts in the water hanging on to the rope and is pulled up just as any stand up skier.

This captivated me. The thrill, the excitement, the rush of being pulled behind a boat; I wanted to try it. My adventurous spirit started stirring. However, participants needed slips signed by their doctors prior to the clinic and participants had to be a year post-injury. I was only about three months post. Damn! Not only did I see a fun, adrenaline rush activity, I met "real" people living with various types of paralysis and disabilities.

I waited an entire year to try it. When the flyer for the two water ski sessions in 1998 arrived in my mailbox, I signed up immediately. The day finally arrived. Starting out a bit cool, it turned warm and sunny in the afternoon, perfect for

Me waterskiing

waterskiing. I grew more excited as I watched the first few people take their turns. At last my turn came. Like stand up waterskiing, it took a few tries to get going. I yelled for the dragger to let go, I surged forward and grabbed the tow rope to free it from the ski. Wow, I was waterskiing again! Three or four times I signaled the boat with a thumb up to go faster, and faster he went. On the first turn, I wiped out two or three times, but fell right out of the cage and floated to the top. Chasers on jet skies also followed the skiers to jump in and help the skier back in the ski. What a rush! On my next turn I wanted to try crossing over the wake.

Momentarily I considered owning my own ski; however, I did not live on a lake, own a speedboat or have friends that did. Skiing twice a year at the clinic would have to suffice. This is an example of the double-edged sword of wheelchair sports. A wide variety of activities and equipment are available, but depending on one's financial or insurance situation, the cost may prohibit participation. Adaptive water skis are not available to rent for a week or the weekend. If one wants to ski at times other than the clinic, it means purchasing one's own ski for about $1,500 to $2,000. As with many wheelchair sports, the equipment is available; being able to afford it is a different story.

In the winter of 1998 I also tried downhill skiing. I downhill skied before my accident and was excited to see I could still do it. And better yet, Cannonsburg ski area here in Grand Rapids had a challenged ski program. My stubbornness did not help me when it came time to suit me up with the right equipment. I had my choice of two pieces of equipment—a mono ski or a bi ski. As the name suggests, the mono ski was one single ski with a seating contraption called a bucket, mounted on it. It sported a lever which raised the bucket up for getting on the chair lift. When the lift came along, the lift seat hit just below the bucket and set the bottom of the bucket on the lift. All of

Downhill skiing

this was done with the assistance of two volunteers who are paired to work with each individual skier.

Then there was the bi ski. This piece provided much more stability as there were two skis side-by-side on which the bucket was mounted. However, it did not have a lever to raise the bucket for the lift, thus I needed more assistance to get on the lift. For both styles of skis, my "poles" were two short skis on short poles called outriggers and one was strapped to each of my arms.

Because I had skied before my accident, I wanted to use the most independent piece of equipment there was—the mono ski. Because of my lack of trunk control, the instructors said it would be very difficult to master because I had no trunk stability or hip movement. I did not care, I wanted to master the mono. The volunteers who worked with me also had me on a tether and would ski behind me and keep my speed controlled so that I did not go flying down the hill.

Well, I did not master the mono ski the first year. Whenever I would attempt a turn, with any slight lean, I fell over. I did not have enough stability to lean only a little when turning. The second year I tried it again, and the third. Still, I remained tethered at the end of each season, unable to master the mono ski. At the beginning of my fourth year, Val, a single amputee who walked with a prosthetic leg and had skied for years, suggested I try the bi ski. Actually, ever since my first year of struggling with the mono ski, she had suggested trying the bi ski. But being stubborn and determined, I would not listen. On the first night of the fourth year she said, "Jocelyn, just humor me and try the bi ski once." I rolled my eyes and begrudgingly agreed.

With this ski I sat a bit lower to the ground. My two volunteers easily loaded me onto the lift, not much differently from the mono ski. While still tethered, I felt much more stable in the bi ski. It enabled me to lean into the turn without falling over. After the first few runs, I got the hang of it. I was skiing again!! Coming off the slopes that evening, I came into the lodge grinning. After all of my resistance and after only one night, I loved the bi ski.

The big joke for that year was that I went bi and loved it. By the end of the season I skied independently and tether-free, still needing assistance onto the lift, of course. It made me realize that in skiing, or any other area where adaptive equipment is needed, it is all about using equipment that allows the greatest degree of independence. How cool you think the equipment looks does not matter if you cannot be independent. Although I've not skied in a few years, I dream of traveling out west to Colorado to ski at resorts stocking the latest and greatest adaptive equipment. Again, it is great that I can still ski, but I cannot go to any ski area like any standing person and rent the equipment I need, so I would need to purchase my own ski for about $2,500. If a ski area rents skis to standing people do they also have to have equipment for seated people? By law yes, but if there is no one requesting it or making an issue of it, the resorts are not going to spend the money on it. There is little enforcement of such a law.

As a skiing mentor, Val wanted more women to play more wheelchair sports in general. Knowing basketball did not appeal to me, she encouraged me for years to try wheelchair tennis. Finally, in June 2000, she persuaded me to join her at tennis practice to check it out. Aside from hitting the ball around on the driveway with my sister, I had never played tennis. Everything about it was new to me. I did not even know how to keep score correctly. My first night on the court, the other players warmly welcomed a new face, especially a female one. They gave me a racquet and showed me what to do. Thankfully, another new quad player had started the week before me so I had a buddy to learn with. He possessed the advantage of having played stand up tennis for most of his able-bodied life. However, we both carried the burden of using everyday chairs and learning new wheelchair skills.

Thankfully, no one documented on tape my first attempt at wheelchair tennis. I had to learn a new skill set for this sport, like pushing the chair while carrying the racquet in my hand, figuring the timing of getting to the ball and hitting it, not to mention the basic task of holding a racquet. Playing in an everyday wheelchair adds an additional challenge too. Sport chairs or tennis chairs are designed for speed and maneuverability, while everyday chairs are designed for comfort and stability. Tennis chairs weigh less—the less weight you have to push the faster you'll go—and have wheels slanting at a 12 to 20 degree angle for stability and turning ease. At the time, the Grand Rapids Wheelchair Sports Association, which helped support the sport, did not have an extra tennis chair available for me to use, so I was stuck with my everyday chair.

Besides meeting some very motivated and fun people who played wheelchair tennis and made me want to return, I loved breaking a sweat and getting my heart pumping. I live an active life, but rarely does my daily activity elevate my heart rate. Even sports like downhill and water skiing did not. My heart may get pumping from the thrill, but not from any sort of cardio workout. I felt tired and a little sore (the good kind of sore) after practice and could not wait to come back the next week.

Since the first clumsy, awkward day, my skill level has greatly improved. I played in my everyday chair for almost a year, then asked my grandparents to help me out with purchasing my very own tennis chair. They agreed and gave me $1,800 toward my chair, which cost around $2,100 then. Today the price is closer to $3,500. Any sort of sporting equipment, even adaptive sporting equipment, is rarely, if ever, covered by health insurance companies. So, most often, people pay out of pocket for their equipment. After finally getting my own chair, I started to compete in wheelchair tennis tournaments, not only here in Grand Rapids, but in tournaments across the country.

Playing tennis

What makes wheelchair tennis one of the greatest sports is its integration level between standing and seated players. The only rule difference in wheelchair tennis is that players are allowed two bounces to hit the ball. The first bounce must land in and the second bounce can be anywhere. We can take the ball out of the air, off one bounce or let it bounce twice before striking it. With that minor rule difference, able-bodied people can play against a wheelchair player or with them on a doubles team. Whatever the arrangement, the seated player still gets two bounces and the standing player gets one. I have played in wheelchair tournaments and I have also played in local, just-for-fun doubles tournaments. As USTA members, wheelchair players can participate in any USTA sanctioned league or tournament.

In 2006 at the Florida Open in Boca Raton, I was reminded of what is so amazing about wheelchair tennis. While it's impressive and jaw-dropping at times to watch world-class players race around the court cranking winners past their opponents, it is most gratifying to see people play simply because they love tennis, especially people who thought they would never play again.

I competed against one such player. Mel, a very friendly black woman from Virginia, was new to wheelchair tennis as a single amputee, but she had played stand up tennis for 20 years. This was her first tournament and she bubbled with enthusiasm. Mel carried a few extra pounds and called everyone "sugar" and "honey." She also hit the ball like a powerhouse. We had a blast playing. After I'd hit a winner by her, she'd exclaim, "Way to play that, sugar!" We played a grueling two and a half hour match in the Florida heat and I claimed victory in our three-set match. As we chatted and packed up our things, she said to me in her sweet Southern accent, "Joce, honey, it has truly been a pleasure meeting you and playing you today. This is just incredible. We had some good points. I'm just so lucky…." and she started crying, overcome with emotion. When the doctors amputated her leg due to some blood clots, she said she never thought she would be on the court again playing a game she loves—and competitively too, not just for fun. Seeing her emotion and her satisfaction made me realize why tennis is great. Some of my other teammates would say winning is the best part and think that I'm too schmaltzy. Aside from the winning, the point is we *can*. We *can* win, lose, play, improve, push ourselves like any other athlete.

In late 2004 an opportunity surfaced for another competition unrelated to sports. One afternoon at work, an e-mail popped into my inbox titled "Now Accepting Applicants for Ms. Wheelchair Michigan." Reluctantly I opened it just to check it out. At this point I had used a chair for nearly eight years, worked within the disability community and had never heard of Ms. Wheelchair Michigan. The e-mail message gave little information other than stating applications could be submitted or contestants could be nominated. After scanning the e-mail, and rolling my eyes I said, "I'm not entering some stupid beauty contest." I then deleted the message. An hour or two later, I received another e-mail entitled, "Someone Has Nominated You to Compete in Ms. Wheelchair Michigan. With a furrowed brow, the words, "What the hell?" fell from my mouth. Now that someone had nominated me, I felt compelled to find out more.

This e-mail provided much greater detail about the pageant,

well, competition actually. The competition began in Michigan in the 1970's. It was for women who used a wheelchair nearly 100 percent of the time for mobility. I make that clarification

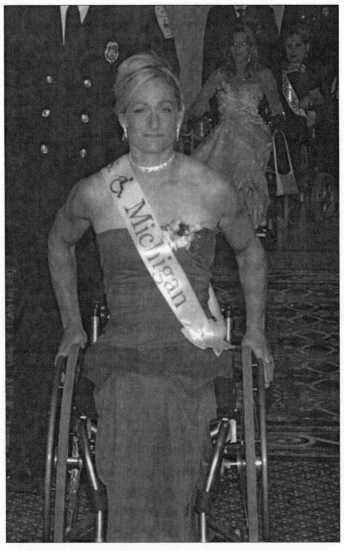

Ms. Wheelchair Michigan

because women use wheelchairs for many reasons, not only for spinal cord injuries or paralysis. Some chair users are able to stand and walk and may not need a wheelchair to move from one place to another. The competition organizers wanted a winner who truly knew about living life in a wheelchair. Contestants also had to be 21 to 60 years of age and marital status was not a consideration. I fit that! Judges rated contestants on speaking ability, level of advocacy and living life despite having a disability. I forwarded the email to Mom and she called me immediately to say I should do it. Being a risk taker with a "let's see where this goes" attitude, I sent in my application and was accepted as a contestant.

In February 2005, the competition took place in the Detroit area. Each contestant had to develop a platform and a message to deliver in her speech for the competition. If she won the title, her message would be the basis for upcoming speeches and appearances. I struggled with finding a platform. One day at work, I asked a co-worker if she noticed anything about me or the way I lived that would be a good message. In my eyes, how I lived my life was ordinary to me and I did not see it as anything special. I needed someone removed from the everyday grind to give me a different perspective. Without hesitation my co-worker replied, "You break the mold for stereotypes and persons with disabilities." So, dispelling the negative stereotypes oppressing persons with disabilities became my message.

The two most often asked questions (and they usually came from men) were: 1) Is there a swimsuit competition, and 2) Is there a talent competition? Thankfully the answer to both questions was no. We wore business attire for interviews with the judges during the day, then changed into evening gowns to deliver our platform speeches for the crowning ceremony. To the applause and cheers of many family and friends in the audience, I was crowned Ms. Wheelchair Michigan 2005.

Yet another accomplishment I felt led to and guided through. And certainly something inconceivable to me lying in a hospital bed in Namibia, Africa.

"Nothing in the world is more dangerous than sincere ignorance and conscientious stupidity."

—Martin Luther King, Jr.

Chapter Thirteen
Ignorance is Not Bliss
(A little Disability 101)

The psychology of disability and adapting to my disability is fascinating—not only observing others' behavior, but also my own thought processes. My accident presented me with a defining before and after moment, occurring within seconds, and giving me a point of reference for comparing experiences. How others see me (or ignore me), interact with me (or not) and watch me offers the starkest comparison. Thank God I do not have any visibly disgusting habits, like picking my nose or digging out ear wax, for all the world to witness.

From the beginning, as a chair user, I was keenly aware that people look at me. They watch me in the grocery store propelling myself and pushing my cart at the same time. They watch me get in and out of my car. When flying to a tennis tournament, they watch me push myself and my tennis chair simultaneously through the airport to catch a flight. Before my accident, I always wanted to be noticed. I felt like I simply blended in and never stood out. Sometimes my friends and I would play these psychological question games and the answers given were meant to reveal something about our personalities. One question was "If you could be an animal, what kind would you be and why?" I always chose a giraffe because they are tall, lean, sleek, and stand out. Well, people certainly notice me now and I only want to blend in.

If given the choice, I would rather be stared at and

acknowledged rather than completely ignored, as if I did not even exist. At least if someone feels uncomfortable around me it means they notice my presence. At times, I can sense people's unease around me. Watching what they do and how they react and interact in situations with me would be a hoot for psychology buffs. OK, I admit it, on rare occasions, because I've been so annoyed with people, I have purposely done things to heighten their feelings of unease.

A women's public restroom sets the scene for a prime example. One of my greatest frustrations is the number of people who do not have a disability, yet nonchalantly use the large wheelchair-accessible stall in the restroom (usually the only one), even when the majority of other stalls are vacant and aplenty. I don't care if there is more room, or if it's down on the end and more private, or the closest one—if you are able-bodied and other stalls are available, the big stalls *are not for you!* On numerous occasions I have entered a nearly vacant restroom only to find the ONE stall I can use occupied by a woman without a disability. While waiting for women to exit the big stall, I have occasionally positioned myself such that they have to really squeeze by me to leave. Often, when seeing me sitting outside waiting for them, the look on their face reveals embarrassment; they know they've been busted. Usually women hurry past me and cannot wait to get out of the restroom. Their level of discomfort is palpable. On one occasion during the winter, a woman was so embarrassed that she left her coat hanging over the stall door and did not even pause to wash her hands.

I also find if I am finished using the bathroom and washing my hands, women coming into the bathroom will not use the big stall, even if there is a line and the big stall is free. If I am present, people will often not use it. Interesting. One of my dream experiments would be to plant a woman without a disability in a restroom for an hour or so to count how many women without disabilities use the big stall. Then put a woman with a disability in the same restroom for an hour to count how many use the big stall. If there is a long line, I have no problem with waiting my turn or people using the big stall. It only grinds me when so many of the smaller stalls are vacant and they choose to use the one stall available to me.

All through high school and college, people often told me, "You would be a good teacher." I did not agree since I had no desire to be in a classroom all day. However, I've learned teaching comes in many forms. While I would not classify myself as a teacher per se, I do educate people all the time about disability. Sometimes the education does take place in a classroom, like when I go to elementary, high school or college classes to talk about living with a disability. Other times it comes in the form of pure example, like living my life and participating in activities people do not expect a person with a disability to do. If I can change the way one person perceives disability, I chalk one up on the "attitude shift" side of life.

It is no big secret that people fear the unknown or unfamiliar. Having a before and after experience—not having, then having a disability—I can understand people's discomfort. However, understanding idiotic, ignorant and insensitive behavior is an entirely different beast. When talking to people, whether in a classroom or business setting, about disability, I encourage people to ask questions. Learning about the unfamiliar has so much power to change someone's attitude. I am very open in talking about disability and tell people, "No matter how politically incorrect you think your question might be, it is more important to ask the question and get the right answer than to assume the wrong answer. We all know what happens when we assume things."

I often hear the question, "how should you treat a person with a disability?" Or I get specific questions like, "Should I kneel down to be at a wheelchair user's level?" or "Should I open the door for them?" First, you should treat a person with a disability as you would treat anyone else. If you are one to make eye contact and smile at people as you pass by, do the same when passing someone with a disability. If you typically open doors for people because it is the polite thing to do, then open the door for someone with a disability. Knowing I am very capable of opening a door and that people simply mean well, it makes me laugh when I approach a building and hear footsteps quicken behind me. I can sense the person rushing to reach the door before me in order to open it for me.

Years ago I removed the push handles from the back of my chair. I learned the hard way that if there is something sticking out from a chair for people to grab hold of and "help" me, they will. I really do not like being pushed because of my poor balance. People do not grasp the treachery of little pebbles, bumps or sidewalk cracks. My front casters are only 4" in diameter and sometimes get caught up on things. So I either maneuver around the obstacle or pop my front wheels up to travel over the obstacle. If people push me, their instinct is to shove the chair with some relative force over the obstacle, but what happens is my chair stops, I do not, and I fly out of my chair. No push handles prevents people from grabbing hold to "help." I see it most when I travel, but it still surprises me how many people go behind me with the intention of pushing me even though I did not request assistance. They end up surprised to find no push handles. Even on my own, I have managed to get caught up on a pebble or a sidewalk crack and fall out of my chair. Thankfully the situation rarely surfaces.

People often ask me if I want help getting my chair in my car. Popping the wheels off and lifting the frame across me to place in the backseat on the passenger side may look rather labor intensive, but it is the norm for me. I typically decline (unless a wheel has rolled away) because it would take too long to explain what to do with my chair. I do not have the patience for that. I have noticed that people offer assistance more often in warm weather than cold weather. If you wonder if someone wants (not needs) help the best thing to do is *ask*. This empowers the person to accept or decline the assistance. Never assume someone needs help simply because of a disability. I try to courteously decline assistance even if I am in a hurry or not in a great mood. My philosophy is that if I snap at or am curt with anyone offering me assistance, that person may leap the conclusion that persons with disabilities are rude and crabby. With an experience like that, the next time that person contemplates offering a person with a disability assistance, he/she will most likely not offer the help because of one bad experience. When in the grocery store, people frequently ask me if I need to get something off a high shelf. Typically I am proactive and ask someone if I do need something; oftentimes I am just looking at the shelf deciding what to purchase.

With years of chair-using experience, I have concluded that people like to help. Sometimes I let them help because I truly need assistance, other times I let them simply because it will make them feel good. In 2007, for a three-week holiday, I returned to New Zealand for two weeks and Australia for one. In the Melbourne, Australia airport on my way back to the States, I was buying water in a little shop. As I packed my wallet away and began to exit the shop, a gentleman approached me. Very politely he asked, "Hi, my name is Billy, do you mind if I ask why you are in the chair?" His southern accent and cowboy hat revealed his American identity. He listened intently and nodded as I told him about my spinal cord injury. As I sized up Billy with his southern accent and tourist ensemble, my intuition kicked in and I knew what was coming next. Very kindly he asked, "Do you mind if I pray over you?" Knowing it would make his day and certainly bring no harm, if not some good, to me, I agreed. Aloud he prayed for me to be healed from my spinal cord injury, that I be able to walk again and that I believe in Him. He then asked if I believed in God. I replied in the affirmative and left to catch my flight.

As I cruised toward my gate, I thought about what just occurred and, more importantly, what constituted healing for people. For Billy, healing meant only getting up out of my chair and walking out of the store. As if my injury and sitting in the chair were the greatest tragedy in my life. Because he did not know me, because he could not see inside my heart, because in *his* eyes a wheelchair symbolized the epitome of tragedy, because of all those reasons and more, he did not know the greatest tragedy in my life is not being able to love myself as the wonderfully gifted woman God made me.

I spent years believing I lacked something or had some major deficit because my dad did not love me in the way that I wanted. Believing (even before using a chair) that something must be horribly wrong with me because the guys I liked did not like me and I never dated much. Not loving myself for who I am, but looking outside of myself for the validation and approval of others to feel loved. Now, that is a tragedy. And it had nothing to do with using a wheelchair.

Since I have not physically gotten up and walked, does it mean I do not have enough faith? That I have not been healed? No. So much healing has taken place since my accident. Healing encompasses so many aspects of one's life, not simply the physical aspects of movement and walking. I have faith in the plan God has for me. Most of the time I am not sure where the plan is taking me, but I seem to be rather comfortable pushing ahead into the unknown. If someone asked me if I wanted to get up and walk, would I say no? Of course not!! Many people travel this earth unhealed and broken. Despite my physical appearance, thankfully, I am not one of them.

After returning from my trip, I popped into the Schuler Books to share my photos with my friend, Denise, and anyone else who may be around. Denise and I had started in the same training class at the bookstore. As I waited for Denise to come out from the back, I browsed through some DVD's and became aware of a man looking at me. I did not know him and I am pretty good with faces and names. As Denise and I chatted and looked at my photos, out of the corner of my eye I noticed two people standing near us. As if cued by a movie director, I stopped talking and in unison she and I turned our heads to the couple on my right. Since she worked there, she asked, "Can I help you?" He looked at me and said, "So, what's the deal?" Playing dumb, I asked, "The deal with what?" I knew what he meant. However, I did not like his approach. I could have thought of ten different ways to have asked me why I use a wheelchair, but honestly, 'what's the deal' was a new one. He replied, "Well, I used one of those things for a while and was almost confined to one."

I simply explained how I acquired a spinal cord injury from sledding down a sand dune. Their eyebrows perked up as if to say, "Really!" Then I added, "That was ten years ago." Again, the eyebrows emphasizing their surprised expressions. For one more wallop I mentioned it happened in Namibia, Africa and now I was sharing photos from my New Zealand and Oz trip. They said, "Well, you certainly get around." And I simply said, "I do what I can." With that, they turned and left. Denise and I turned to each other with a what-the-fuck look and started laughing, partly out of surprise, partly out of disbelief in the guy's lack of social tact.

Another favorite story is the Home Expo incident. Disability Advocates started a program called ZeroStep in July 2005. As the name suggests, it is about promoting zero step entrances for residential homes and the use of universal design features throughout all homes. ZeroStep is not about disability, it is about building a home that is livable for you and welcoming for family and friends. One evening at a Home Expo show in Grand Rapids, I was working our ZeroStep display. As people passed by I would tell them about our display and why universal design is the wave of the future in home design. This one couple around the age of 60 paused in front of the booth. I gave my brief spiel about universal design. The gentleman looked at me, looked at the display, then back at me again and asked, "So, are you really in that thing or are you part of the display?"

I paused, not exactly sure how to react. I knew his question was genuine, although asked in a tactless manner. In a roundabout way, he paid me a compliment. Obviously I did not fit into any stereotype he possessed of what a wheelchair user should look like. I responded with, "What!?? Yes, of course I'm really in a chair. That would be awful for someone to fake it for advertising purposes." We still chuckle about that one around the office anytime we set up a display at any Home Expo show.

Truth be told, I would still rather have a person ask a genuine question in a tactless way than make assumptions about me and my life. However, genuine questions asked in a respectful manner are my preference. It comes down to respect for other people. If you treat people with respect, then treat persons with disabilities with respect. Most of my stories have been about the ignorance and social ineptness of adults. Children have supplied me with an entirely different and wonderful treasure trove of stories.

One of my favorites took place at tennis practice during the winter at the local indoor club. One of the tennis coaches at the club also refereed the Midwest Wheelchair Tennis tournament in Grand Rapids. All of his children played tennis. The coach and his nine year-old son were packing up their things as we started to come on the court to get in our chairs and get ready to play. The coach knew us and felt comfortable, the son seemed a bit uneasy. They were standing about six feet from me and the boy asked his dad, "Did they all break their legs or are they in them (the wheelchairs) just for fun?" The dad gave the perfect answer, "I don't know, why don't you ask her?" as he pointed to me. So I smiled at the boy, trying not to laugh. His question exemplified how a child's mind works: broken leg = wheelchair. Maybe he had only seen someone in a wheelchair who broke their leg. I answered, "Actually, none of us broke our legs. Most of us injured our backs and spinal cords so that we cannot walk anymore. Some of us lost a leg or part of a leg and cannot run and play stand up tennis, but we can play wheelchair tennis." The boy nodded his head, satisfied with the answer.

In addition to asking questions, some kids discover and learn by touching. Once, while in a home improvement store, I was cruising down the aisle and about to pass a father and his son who looked to be about four years old. As the boy passed me, he ran his hand right over the rubber of my tire. At the time my tires had a pretty thick tread and texture. They must have looked fascinating to the kid and he simply wanted to see what they felt like. I do not even know if the father noticed. If he did, he did not tell his son "Don't do that or don't touch that." Pulling a child away for asking a question about something foreign to them or touching something new, merely teaches the child to stay away from whatever "it" is. Picture this, a child asks a stranger, "Why do you have that wheelchair?" The parent, pulls the child away apologizing to the person in the chair and the child receives no answer. With the person in the chair being rather intriguing, the child has just learned that, 1) the person in the chair is different (without being told why) and, given that I was just yanked away, 2) I need to stay away from people who are different like that. Asking questions is okay. If the person does not want to answer them, he or she will more than willingly tell you so.

I worked with a rather odd duck named Alex at the bookstore. He was tall, thin, with dark curly hair and wanted only to write. His aloofness intrigued me, as it did many girls. We had some good chats, especially on the pre-car evenings when I had to wait for the bus to pick me up. The day I told him I graduated from the University of Michigan with a degree in English Literature vividly sticks in my mind. He laughed in my face. Apparently I did not fit his vision of what a U of M English major should look like. He once remarked, "You are so lucky that you get to collect disability and not work much." Being Alex, his comment did not offend me. He continued, "I would love to have more time to write and create." Taking to heart my Oscar Wilde quote I cautioned him, "Be careful Alex, you just may get your wish, but it won't come the way you want it. What if you got to collect disability, but had a brain injury and had the awareness of what you used to be able to do, but can no longer formulate words or string thoughts together?"

Spinal cord injuries and paralysis encompass so much more than merely not walking or not feeling. Seeing someone in a chair, especially a manual wheelchair, people often leap to the conclusion the chair user is paralyzed from the waist down. After reading my story, you know the conclusion is assumptive. The loss involved with paralysis extends far beyond not walking. It encompasses the loss of feeling someone touch my leg or stroke my lower back, the loss of bladder and bowel function, and the loss of muscle movement.

Because my T-5 injury left me without use of my abdominal muscles, I have no muscles through my torso to help push air out. Therefore, my sneezes are very dainty, high pitched and sometimes nearly inaudible. Coughing is difficult which makes having a simple cold exhausting. In order to put pressure on my abdomen I usually have to lean/ throw myself forward a bit and put an arm across my stomach to cough. Even blowing my nose requires a magnitude of energy. Getting a cold now kicks my ass. I reckoned it may simply be my age, but putting so much effort into sneezing, coughing and blowing my nose quickly zaps my energy.

One thing I miss the most is my laugh. Sure, I still laugh now, but it sounds nothing like before my accident because my muscles cannot contract and push the air out as they did before. My laugh was rather infectious, the sort of laugh which made others laugh, especially when I really got going and could not stop laughing. It's these small things people never consider when thinking about paralysis.

Like filling my car up with gas. Instead of going through the whole process of getting my chair out, I usually wait until I have a friend with me so she can hop out of the car and fill up my tank. Going to Costco is great because an attendant is always out by the pumps and will assist me pumping gas. Shaving my legs is something else to think about. I used a manual handheld razor just after my accident, but soon changed to an electric razor. Not too long ago, I used a manual handheld razor again and wondered why I stopped. Originally I thought it was because my legs flopped around too much and it was too difficult to try to balance myself, hold my leg and shave it all at once. But after a few times with the handheld razor, I remembered I stopped because I could never gauge how much pressure I applied when dragging the razor across my leg. I nicked myself up quite a bit, especially with a slightly dull razor.

About five years after my accident, an electronic stimulation clinic in Cleveland, Ohio invited me to participate in a panel discussion on electronic stimulation at their annual international conference. The panel was comprised of eight people, a few paras and a few quads, both of varying degrees of "ability." One was a complete quad who used a ventilator and a power chair. Since he could not move even a finger to operate a power chair he wore a retainer type device in his mouth. By running his tongue along the roof of his mouth and hitting certain spots on the device, he could maneuver his power chair.

The session facilitator asked the panel members what bodily functions they would like improved or restored. The number one answer was bladder/bowel function. The facilitator wrote the list for everyone to see. Surprisingly, walking ranked 7 or 8 on the list. In selecting one or two functions to regain, we panelists seriously considered what would improve our quality of life most. The mere act of standing ranked higher than walking. From a practical perspective, being able to stand would facilitate so many things—reaching items on shelves, standing to stretch and getting into higher vehicles like SUVs. However, for the quads, many simply want the use of their hands restored, screw walking.

If you are in a crowded place and someone needs to pass by you, do you step aside a few inches to give them just enough room to pass, or do you back up several inches or feet to give the person plenty of room? If you were to pass by someone in a rather large, but deserted hallway, do you take a step or two to the side as you pass, or do you cross to the other side of the hallway to avoid the person? From what I remember as a walking person, most people, in both instances, moved just enough to give me a bit of room to pass. As a wheelchair user, I notice a monumental difference. No matter how crowded a place, getting through the crowd for me is like parting the Red Sea. Once people see a person in a wheelchair, they typically back *way* up to move from my path. Rarely do people move just the few inches required to allow me to get through. Without knowing it, instinctively they back away from the chair.

Even passing people in hallways, especially ones with plenty of room, people most often step away a few feet rather than the few inches I would need to pass them. And sometimes, they even stop completely, practically clinging to the wall as I pass by. I am sure most are unaware of their behavior. If they are aware, they probably think they are giving me plenty of room, but all I sense from that is a fear of being near a person in a chair. The icing on the cake is whether or not, after backing up a great deal to allow me room to pass, the person makes eye contact and acknowledges me or simply pretends I do not exist.

"I believe, Fate smiled and Destiny
Laughed as she came to my cradle, 'know this child
will be able.'
Laughed as she came to my mother, 'know this child
will not suffer'
Laughed as my body she lifted, 'know this child will
be gifted with love, with patience and with faith. She'll
make her way.'"

—*Wonder* by Natalie Merchant

CHAPTER FOURTEEN

MOVING FORWARD

From the beginning I wondered how I should conclude my story. I'm not dying at the end. I've not experienced any miraculous get-up-out-of-the-chair healing. However, it does not mean miracles and healing have not occurred.

Not being much of a planner or goal setter, my approach to life has been a "let's do it and see what happens" attitude. Otherwise known as "by the seat of my pants." Not to be mistaken for sitting back on the sidelines and waiting idly for opportunities to come my way or be handed to me. Oh, no. By choice, I am always trying new things to see what fits me best. As a kid I tried little league softball, ballet dancing, gymnastics, ice skating and basketball. In junior high and high school, I tried volleyball, downhill skiing, cheerleading, cross country and track. Into my adult years I bought a guitar, took lessons and discovered I did not have any hidden musical talent. More crucially, after my accident, I continued to explore new avenues like taking a drawing class (no hidden talent there either, rats!), playing various wheelchair sports, sky diving, working in the nonprofit world and wandering along my spiritual path. This time to truly find my direction and purpose in life, I have taken many leaps with many unknowns in my future. If all the experiences of the past mold us into who we are today, my momentum did not and does not allow me to stop.

The years since my accident have shown me the wondrous, miraculous things possible in life. Lying paralyzed at the bottom of a sand dune on the other side of the world, I did not know

255

what to expect life to be like. In the midst of rehab and learning to do everything all over again as a paralyzed person, I grasped no concept of what life would really be like "on the outside." I would say my life is normal, but what does that mean? In their own worlds, everyone's life is normal. Every day I use a wheelchair and do not walk. Some things I do very differently than a walking person, but many of the things I do the same. And when life presents physical barriers I cannot manage, I get one of those walking people to help or carry me.

My life is full and good. However, it did not all magically happen. It took and still takes work. At times when I did not "feel" like doing things like going to my dad's wedding reception, going back to church, or heck, even just going out with friends, I made a decision—sometimes conscious sometimes subconscious—about how to live my life. Looking for the good, even on bad days and in bad situations, is not always easy, but I choose to do it.

Over ten years ago I heard a story on National Public Radio (NPR) which truly made an impact on how I live my life. It was simply about a mailbox and a snowplow, yet packed a doozy of a life lesson at the end. Consider yourself lucky if you have never experienced a winter with heavy snow and the joy of the commercial snowplow clearing your road. In my neighborhood, when the plows swung through the streets, they left an enormous pile of heavy, packed snow at the end of each driveway which usually had to be cleared with a shovel instead of a snow blower. In the story on NPR, this neighborhood had a problem with mailboxes getting hit with the side of the plow. Two guys lived across the street from each other, each had their mailboxes and posts, knocked over and broken more than once. One neighbor tried to devise a system with the most rigid, sturdy post and mailbox, but the plow still knocked it over. The other neighbor devised a system in which the mailbox rested on a flexible, springy post. The plow still came by and knocked over the mailbox, but it sprang back up after the plow passed. The point? Success in life is more readily achieved with flexibility and adaptability than rigidity.

I've learned to live more with what is rather than looking back at what was or looking ahead to what might be. No one can predict the future with 100 percent certainty. Even if one could, would I believe? Probably not. If someone told me on April 12, 1997 that it would be my last day as a walking woman, I would have laughed because it sounded so ludicrous. By telling me to turn on the TV broadcast of wheelchair basketball, Dr. Schroder tried to show me how full and active my life could be, despite paralysis. While in Namibia or at Mary Free Bed, if someone told me I would become a fundraiser, take up wheelchair tennis and write a book, I would have labeled them as "crazy" and disregarded their prediction. Although uncertain about what I would do, those three things did not even appear on the radar screen.

Before the age of 30, I experienced unimaginable events, both tragic and good. My accident, my parents' divorce and the demise of my family hold high rankings on the tragic list. Conversely, traveling around the world, the fundraiser after my accident and still participating in adventurous activities (skydiving, skiing) hold high rankings on the good list.

The transformation of my family falls on both lists. In 2006 if someone had told me that in the next few years I would begin spending holidays with all the Dettloffs reunited, with my mom being around my dad without any bitterness or anger, I would have said it will be a cold day in hell before that happened. Well, I do not think the temp has dropped in Hades, but today, those scenarios do occur and even with the presence of my parents' significant others. What prompted the big change? My dad's divorce from his second wife. After so many years, Mom felt validated and realized she was not to blame for their divorce. Dad and I have made an effort to rebuild our relationship. We still have our challenges, but he is my dad and always will be. Letting go and moving on truly ushers in new life.

With my education, travels, career choice, even this book, my faith in not only God, but faith in things working out as they are meant to gives me confidence and strength to move forward without a final destination in sight. Without knowing it, these seeds have been in me since birth. In going through such a life-altering trauma, I am still very much who I was before my accident. Sure I have changed since my accident. Many of us change over the years. Are any of us the same person in our 30's as we were in our 20's? God I hope not. But there is a difference between one's spirit being changed and being broken. My back was broken, not my spirit, not my will and not my essence.

I do not know what my life will look like in a month, in a year or in ten years. I dream and hope it will look a certain way or particular things occur. Very little, if anything, in my life has turned out as I imagined so many years ago as a child, a teenager, a college student and a world traveler. But as I'm prone to do, I'll keep moving forward, encountering both expected and unexpected joys and challenges along the way. And I'll see what happens.

Chapter Fifteen
Meg's Letter

A few years after my accident, I began questioning what specifically happened on the day of my accident. What happened as people watched me come down the dune? How far did I sail through the air? What were others thinking? I know, you may think these questions would have popped up much sooner, but I can be a bit slow sometimes. Remember, I am the tortoise.

I contacted those I kept in touch with to provide me with their versions of what happened that day. Here is the letter Meg mailed her parents within days after the accident. I've read it many times over the years. Thankfully I possess an account of what happened at the very beginning to always remind me how far I have come.

Hi Jocelyn,

Well you asked for it here it is, didn't realise I'd written quite so much... I've simply written the lot, even after you left, I hope it doesn't make you cry. It'd made me shed a couple.

Dear Ma and Pa

What I am about to write is my most awful experience yet in my years of travelling.

After sunrise at Sessriem we went to Dune 45 with the sandboards, before the pax ascended I warned them not to descend a slope with a sharp angle at the bottom, instead I suggested that a gradual gradient is a better option. Up they went.

I could see the boarders at the top and could see they weren't at the best spot so kept trying to point to a safer decline, an instruction obviously unseen, as, soon they were descending exactly where they shouldn't. Matt was the first to descend and descend at speed did he! Fortunately he noticed that the end would be dangerous so bailed out rolling down the dune a couple of times. The next thing you know another passenger is following, why he didn't wait for the all clear I have no idea and he hit the ground with immense speed rolling over and over again. We then began to yell and wave our arms in protest against the rest's descent but although they saw us they kept coming hitting the ground at speed. We managed to discover that they were OK but shaken and bruised, we then yelled and yelled waving our arms and were absolutely amazed to see another descend, Jocelyn.

Some people turned and couldn't look (I remember Paula) while I yelled and yelled until my lungs hurt "DIG YOUR FEET IN DIG YOUR FEET IN, TOUCH TOUCH, DIG YOUR FEET IN" and she kept coming if only she had bailed out like Matt. Then at the bottom she hit a lump that had been hit by the others @ great speed and somersaulted right up into the air then tumbled to a stop. Matt and I immediately ran to her SCREAMING AND YELLING to the others not to come down, finally they took heed of our pleas. Jocelyn lay on her back, her eye was badly bruised but she seemed completely with it. I asked her if she hurt anywhere? "I can't feel my legs." She said. I pinched her in a few spots - no, no feeling. I felt for broken bones, none but she could feel nothing right up to her breast bone and needless to say she couldn't move.

I immediately instructed Matt to go back to Sessriem to a

lodge and arrange for an airlift out, first though we erected the cook tent for shelter and he left plenty of water. Matt was clearly very shaken and left with great speed - though I told him to be careful. All we could do was wait.

I told Jocelyn exactly what was happening and that we maybe waiting for some time. We made every effort to keep her still and not move her a bit. It was so weird, I truly felt like I was on stage acting out a scene and Jocelyn was "playing" the victim. Let me tell you she did a star performance as a patient, more than a performer would be capable of. She was so incredibly calm. Kathy a school teacher kept asking her questions "how many brothers and sisters do you have?" etc, good teacher questions, in a way treating Jocelyn like a child, but she was very comforting, if I were in that position I wouldn't want anyone else talking to me.

Everyone was sitting in the cook tent, about 10 of us not really talking but staring out into the vast desert as the wind picked up. Soon we had to sit on the edges of the tent as it threatened to lift. There were soon a few cars in the distance, tourists coming to see the dune. I went up to them with another passenger, Paula, to ask if anyone had any medical training, we were worried that maybe she had punctured her lung as she complained about tightness around the chest and her breathing seemed to become more laboured. When describing the situation to the tourists they seemed totally shocked. And rightly so the situation was very serious, but no there were no medics amongst them. I worried thinking about her lungs filling up with blood and not wanting to tip her on her side because of the suspected injury.

Like a fairy God Father a doctor soon arrived, Herbert from Germany. He inspected her condition, he probably wasn't the best doctor in the world as his Germanic manner was blunt and seemingly unconcerned (perhaps a cultural difference and a harsh judgment from me) but he did let us know that her lung wasn't punctured and yes she did have a back injury, there wasn't anything he could do without a hospital and assured us that we had done the best thing possible. We had to wait. Somehow I already knew this. God it had all happened so quickly. Now look at the situation! I asked him if he could take some of the passengers back to camp, there was no need for everyone to sit in helpless windy silence. So we were then 5 plus Jocelyn. Jocelyn had been so brave. I have no idea how she remained so calm. She never really opened her eyes but kept moving her forearms and clenched and released her fists saying "Oh God I just want to move"

Almost immediately after the others left the wind really picked up. I was sitting on the cook tent tarp with my back to the wind and it was lifting me off the ground. Sand was sweeping in gusts into the blue tent and covering Jocelyn, she calmly closed her eyes and let the sand drift over her. Paula, her friend, did her best to protect Jocelyn's face with the clothes we'd donated

I only weighing 52kg [115 lbs] had to swap sides of the tent as I couldn't hold it down. So Kathy a more hefty lady took my spot. And the wind continued. In the tent was Thierry, Jean Marie, Kathy, Paula, myself and Jocelyn lying helpless in the sand. Calm and strong, twitching her hands and forearms at intervals, Paula sat over Jocelyn smoothing her hair while Paula's own cascaded over her shoulders. She had my shirt wrapped around Jocelyn's head to cover it from the sand and held her hand when Jocelyn wasn't twitching and saying "Oh God I want to move" the rest of us held the tent and covered our own heads when the sand blew in gales into the blue refuge. Jean Marie held the tent with his hand and stood staring into the distance, he spoke no English so we did not really communicate at this very point but I imagine he was staring and waiting for that help to arrive.

Our conversations were small short lived and an attempt albeit futile to make as much light of the situation as we could. Kathy asked what Jocelyn's favourite ski resort was, had she ever been a bridesmaid? Jocelyn answered all questions as if she were at the pub. What must have been going through her head?

Soon the clouds came in and out in the middle of the oldest desert in the world it rained and rained and rained. It was like a scene from Shakespeare's plays where weather plays the mood, where things weren't in their place. Again I equated the situation in my head to a strange scene on stage, I couldn't help it. At least the rain would hold some of the sand in place. We continued to stare across the vast desert surrounded by giant dunes, feeling very small.

We sat in eerie semi silence for 3 long, long hours before we were finally broken from the silence by the presence of an aeroplane. FINALLY help was here. The sky was still very grey and now the wind had picked up again. I was the first to spot the plane, I could see the lights in the distance and as it grew nearer and nearer I begged that it wasn't a group of sight see'ers. It soon disappeared behind the dune and my fears were enhanced. I hoped it was just looking for a place to land, but I couldn't hear it any longer. Soon though it reappeared and came closer and closer... I remember seeing on the movies people waving at planes to let them know where they and honestly that's what prompted me to do so too! Strange. So I stood outside of the tent crisscrossing my arms in the air. The plane then swooped down over us and I could see the red cross on the planes belly THANK GOD.

It was such an emotional sight seeing the plane fly so low over the cook tent it was all I could do not to cry. Then it swooped away again and over another series of dunes. For God's sake LAND! We were all thinking but knew it must have been looking for a safe place. The wind was getting strong and the sand was in the air. The plane circled and circled so many times that Jocelyn began to show her first real signs of distress, "Its been over 6 times now, why wont it land?" We tried to assure her that it would soon, it was just looking for a suitable spot, but we were thinking the same thing. Matt had returned with the truck by that stage and apparently was almost beside himself with worry and had a hard time dealing with rationality, as the plane circled and circled one of the passengers, Ross, stood on the roof with a pair of my underpants as a wind sock trying to indicate where the wind was blowing and Matt nearly took off with Ross on the roof as he wanted to chase the plane.

Finally 20 LONG minutes later the plane landed on the road and Matt brought the doctor with special stretcher and medicines over. He looked shaken, really shaken. I'm not sure if he has ever had to deal with a crisis before and this certainly wasn't easy breaking ground.

The doctor went through the normal procedures of introducing himself then went about putting Jocelyn on a drip. The wind had now died, still I was gripping onto the tent as if in a gale and realised I could let go and in a way, I realised I could let go of Jocelyn, she was in the doctors hands now.

I then had to organize a companion for her, I wanted to go myself but I still had 21 other people to take to Cape Town, Matt hadn't done the trip before so that was up to me. So I *spoke to Jocelyn's friend Paula and to Matt. Obviously Matt for responsibility reasons would have to go and only one could go at the time so Paula would have to catch up. I also warned both of them that it was going to be difficult as they may be there when the doctor told her she might never walk again. They both looked very shocked and rightly so but somehow I don't think they REALLY thought about the consequences until then. Sometimes I'm too damned logical. I'd been thinking about these consequences, how will the group react, how Jocelyn will finally react when it sinks in - what has happened, how will her family feel. I never once thought of myself. A lot of people seemed numb trying not to think of the worst, but hoping she'd bruised her spinal cord and would be OK in few weeks. I tried very hard to believe this too, but By 4:00 PM, 4 hours after the accident Matt, with Jocelyn flew to Windhoek to casualty.*

Upon my return I had an immediate battle with Jocelyn's insurance company. Matt had phoned them earlier to inform of the accident, they then told him that they would not allow authorisation for an airlift until a doctor had been to the site 45 kms [28 miles] away, returned and reported the conditions. Matt overrode this - Good on him and organised the airlift leaving one of the passengers to battle with the red tape. A doctor was in the lodge later and after being described the situation from the passenger confirmed the urgency. The insurance company then said they wanted the medivac company to radio phone the USA from the accident site "I'm sorry sir but we don't have such telecommunication in Namibia" to which the response was "Where's that?!"

So when I came in that night I had to relay details to the insurance company about date of birth address etc, all of which

I didn't have on me at the time, so I had yet another phone call that went around in circles and achieved nothing. I'm not sure if this upset me because I was stressed or if it was a genuinely poorly run operation. In the end I hung up on them, then phoned operations in England, broke them the news, and let them take it from there.

After my stressful phone call Phil took me under his wing and gave me a beer, he likes his beer. I then went back to the truck to officially address the group. I said it was a terrible thing that had happened out on the dunes and how I had sent Matt with Jocelyn to Windhoek for medical attention...."This is not an easy thing for any of us but I'm sure Jocelyn would not want you to be gloomy for the rest of the trip, she was very strong out there and showed a spirit we could all learn a few lessons from. So let's keep our chins up and continue as best we can..." I half said this for myself as I knew I'd find it hard, as rational as I was I knew soon I'd feel bad. And I did. I slept well mainly because I was exhausted mentally and physically, but now I was to lead the trip solo so had to focus.

The following day was a long trip across the Namib desert a very straight road allowing plenty of time to think. I could think of nothing else. I went over everything again and again trying to keep my spirits up for the group and head level to lead. It was hard work but I did it. We were headed to Luderitz, a German town on the edge of Namibia a once lucrative diamond mining area. I was exhausted by the time I got there. I kept hoping and hoping that the outcome of the accident wouldn't be the worst but I think my subconscious had already diagnosed the situation. Still you never knew. I had called the hospital that morning to get at report, I knew they wouldn't be able to tell me much and they didn't, except that she was in intensive care with bad back injuries but was fine. I'd spent all day going over every word "bad" "back" (not spine?) injuries (why plural?) "fine" (no complications? Cut and dry? She can't walk?)

I dreaded the phone call I finally made to operations England, and by the soft tone of Boomers voice I knew he was about to tell me bad news.

"Its not good, it looks like she won't walk again, she's damaged her spinal cord.." I was numb and became suddenly very rational again.

"Is that definite?"

"Yep pretty much."

"How's Matt?"

"He's fine."

"How's Jocelyn's spirit"

"She's coping very well apparently, her mother is flying out on Friday, she needs an operation then will probably fly back to the states..."

We then went on to discuss other work matters and I hung up. I then had to pay for my telephone call and it was the hardest thing. My eyes suddenly filled with tears, I couldn't talk, think or hardly speak, but I did manage to get a receipt for the phone call for my accounts. I walked out the door into the fresh blustery air of Luderitz with tears streaming down my face, I'd finally given into my heart that was screaming with pent up emotion.

But soon again my head took over and as I walked to the edge of the road, looking over the sea, I kept telling myself, you have to be strong, I kept thinking about the group, soon I had to tell them that Jocelyn could no longer walk. Deep breath, control, shoulders straight, and I walked back to the truck. I met a couple of the passengers walking down the road en route to a hotel for the night. I couldn't bring myself to tell them right them so made a casual joke and arranged a time to meet them the next day and continued on. Soon another passenger Annabel - a dear lovely person- came up to me and asked if I had any news. I nodded my head and tears immediately streamed down my face, she didn't need to ask any further questions and it took seconds for her face also to be covered. We sat on a wall near the truck and were soon comforted by Ross - a fabulous passenger, very kind and supportive. I let the tears stream for a while, its only natural and felt I shouldn't deny myself completely, but again sucked them back in and hopped into the truck to break the news to the rest of the group. From my face I think they had already guessed, my voice was shaky when I told them. There was an awful silence that swept over the truck and tears streamed down many cheeks. Then I drove to the campsite, in control by then (I thought) and very rationally told them where the toilets were, where to put their tents and what was happening the following day. People milled off the truck and were soon coming up to me and hugging me " Oh God don't do that, I'm going to cry again," I said and did, we all did, we needed to.

It rained in the desert that day.

There you have it, not sure what you will make of this bit nervous to be honest sending it to you but there you have it. Hope it has shed another light on the out of place day.

Love Meg

Acknowledgements

Sitting here writing the Acknowledgements section, it is hard to believe my book is done. It has been a long, thoughtful, emotional and gratifying process. So many people have played a part in making this book a reality. Since my accident first happened, many people have said, "Wow, you have a fascinating story, you should write a book." I would first like to thank Rosemary Gardiner who gave me the strongest and most enthusiastic encouragement from the very beginning.

Thank you to all of my draft readers—Ann Matchinsky, Denise Taylor, Lynn Antisdel, Pamela Accetta Smith, Lynn Bender, Jane Wheaton, Mary Moran, Cathy Sumeracki, Eunice Cox, Patrick Murray, Christa Blackman, Elizabeth Van Ark, Cindy Lanning Burch, Jackie Justice Brown and Raymond Wlodkowski—your time, comments and critiques contributed to this masterpiece.

I am very grateful for a happenstance encounter on a random Friday morning with Dan Pierson. He has assisted me in countless ways through this process and was a true cheerleader who believed in me every step of the way.

Meg Hall and Matt Varley, to say this book could not have been written without your help, both in and out of Africa, is an understatement.

Thank you to Dragoman for giving me the opportunity to experience the most rustic adventure of my life. And for supplying me with some photographs for this book.

Cheers to David Briggs and Colin Sullivan, because they would never forgive me if I did not mention them once in my book.

Thank you to everyone who kept asking me over the years, "How is your book coming?" It kept me on track.

Special thanks to my family whose support has helped me thrive. You have played a huge role in getting me to where I am today and in shaping the person I am.

About the Author

Jocelyn Dettloff grew up in Kalamazoo, Michigan and graduated from the University of Michigan with a degree in English Literature. She loves traveling, playing tennis, reading, seeking adventure and being an eternal student of the lessons life has to teach her. She lives in Grand Rapids, Michigan. This is her first book.